SHAKE SHACK

SHAKE SHACK

Recipes & Stories
Randy Garutti & Mark Rosati

Introduction by Danny Meyer

Produced by Dorothy Kalins Ink
Photographs by Christopher Hirsheimer and Melissa Hamilton
Design by Don Morris Design

Copyright © 2017 by Shake Shack Enterprises, LLC
Principal photographs copyright © 2017
by Christopher Hirsheimer

First published in the United States by Clarkson
Potter/Publishers, an imprint of the
Crown Publishing Group, a division of
Penguin Random House LLC, New York.

First published in the UK in 2017 by Sphere

ISBN 978-0-7515-7109-7

Cover design by Don Morris Design
Cover photographs by Hirsheimer & Hamilton
Endpapers: Evan Sung (front) and
Christopher Hirsheimer (back)

For additional photography credits, see page 235.

10 9 8 7 6 5 4 3 2 1

The moral right of the author has been asserted.

A CIP catalogue record for this book is available
from the British Library.

Printed and bound in Barcelona by Liberdúplex SL
Papers used by Sphere are from well-managed forests
and other responsible sources.

MIX
Paper from
responsible sources
FSC® C104740

Sphere
An imprint of
Little, Brown Book Group
Carmelite House
50 Victoria Embankment
London EC4Y 0DZ

An Hachette UK Company
www.hachette.co.uk

www.littlebrown.co.uk

Table of Contents

Chapter

1

Born in a Hot Dog Cart

Success Was Accidental; The Idea Was Not

By Danny Meyer

People always talk about how Shake Shack happened by accident. But it didn't really. I had read Billy Shore's book, *The Cathedral Within,* about the human desire to build something far bigger than ourselves, something that would outlive us. What he proposed was a new way to think about building broader community wealth through capitalism. And right from the beginning I saw the hot dog cart in a public park, and Shake Shack itself, as a "community wealth venture."

We agreed to do the cart in Madison Square Park (MSP) in 2001, as part of a Public Art Fund project by the Thai artist Navin Rawanchaikul, called I ❤ TAXI. The artist conceived a working hot dog cart to accompany giant taxi cabs on stilts. We decided it would be interesting to explore whether our idea of "enlightened hospitality" could work for something as simple as a hot dog cart. That's why we served only Chicago-style and Taxi dogs, because if you give people a choice of eight toppings, hospitality dictates you'd have to remember their preferences! We promised to donate 100% of our profits to the Park, which was sort of easy since we lost money in years one and two.

Danny celebrates the opening of the Shack in the Park, with hizzoner, Mayor Mike Bloomberg, 2004.

I've said we made $7,500 in year three. Actually, we didn't. I was just so embarrassed that we'd lost money for three years, we chose to make a bigger contribution. After three summers of operating the hot dog cart, we collaborated with the City of New York, the Parks Department, and the Madison Square Park Conservancy to imagine and build a permanent kiosk.

The idea was we'd raise the money philanthropically; the Park would be the landlord, the kiosk would create a reason for people to use the park and thus keep it safe: community wealth. Today, we know the role Shake Shack had in developing the Madison Square Park neighborhood. There's not a real estate proposal that goes out that doesn't tout us as a neighbor. We're proud that today the Park makes serious money from Shake Shack.

@beeblegum

"Who ever wrote the rule that fast food can't be great food?"

—DANNY MEYER

The world of full-service fine dining is the world most of our leaders came from. They grew up with a certain level of sophistication. That's the reason Shake Shack tastes different, looks different, and feels different. It's an important distinction to make. If you look at the history of restaurant chains, they began with a business mentality and a financial skill set—a mechanical process for replication and scale. It's almost impossible to retrofit a fine dining mindset into that skill set, but we've learned that it is possible to develop and inject that skill set into a pre-existing fine dining mentality.

Shake Shack became a petri dish for our company, Union Square Hospitality Group. It was a place for our people to experiment with how we might learn to scale our philosophy of enlightened hospitality.

What is "fine casual"? As I once said in a talk I gave at TEDxManhattan, no change has floored me more than the convergence of fine dining and casual dining. Fine casual means appropriating the cultural priorities that fine dining, at its best, believes in. It's a whole new way of balancing the equation of quality, price, and time. With fine casual you get nearly all the quality: you're willing to give up some of the niceties of service (no reservations, no servers, or tablecloths, or flowers), but you'll get 100% of the same food we would source—the same excellent beef, the same fine chocolate. You'll save about 80% of the money you'd spend, and about 60% of the time.

Right place, right time. When the permanent Shack in Madison Square Park opened in 2004, it was a watershed year for restaurants in New York City. Legendary French restaurants were closing fast, but the food world wasn't going backward on quality; we wanted to go forward without pomp or frills. Daniel Boulud's db Bistro had added super-gourmet burgers; Momofuku Noodle Bar opened that year with high culinary aspirations and

Since 1870, art was a part of
Madison Square Park. Left, The
Statue of Liberty's right arm,
in 1876; above, I ♥ TAXI sculpture
by Nabin Rawanchaikul in 2001.

no backs on their stools. Gastropubs like The Spotted Pig opened,
and even we were experimenting with bringing refined cooking
to bar dining with our new restaurant at MoMA, The Modern.
Our world was ripe for a place like Shake Shack.

Burgers! People wondered why they never thought of doing a
really great burger in the guise of a quick-serve restaurant (not
that it's particularly quick to wait in that line). We just got lucky.
As the late Josh Ozersky wrote in *Esquire*: "Shake Shack took the
ultimate American trash food and approached it not as an object
for postmodern reinterpretation, but as a *dish to be executed.*"

Round Two was bigger than Round One. At USHG, we
had never even thought of doing anything for the second time.
Anything! People said "You've gotta do another one." And I
said "But we don't DO other ones!" I was urging slow, slow, slow
growth. I was the emergency brake. But the second Shake Shack

The Original Menu Sketch

Just Imagine:
Our Name
Could've Been …

FROSTEE SHAKE
or
MADISON MIXER
or
PARKING LOT
or
CUSTARD'S FIRST STAND
or
DOG RUN
or
CUSTARD PARK

FROSTEE SHAKE   PARKING LOT   DOG RUN
MADISON MIXER   CUSTARD'S FIRST STAND   CUSTARD PARK

GRIDDLE

HAMBURGER   (DOUBLE)

CHEESEBURGER   ,,

KETCHUP, MUSTARD, LETTUCE
PICKLES, ONIONS, SPORT PEPPER

TUNA BURGER   BRIOCHE BUN   GINGER

MUSHROOM BURGER
   W/ CHEESE

CRINKLE CUT
FRENCH FRIES

CHEESE FRIES W/ SPORT PEPPERS

STEAM

CHICAGO DOG
   POPPY BUN

N.Y. DOG

10 Toppings
(PICKLES, TOMATOES, ONION, SPORT PEPPERS, RELISH, CEL. SALT,
KETCHUP, MUSTARD, LETTUCE) CUCUMBER
(SAUERKRAUT, Red onion relish
   TOMATO/ONIONS, KETCHUP, MUSTARD)

FROZEN CUSTARD

CONES   VANILLA
SUNDAES   CHOCOLATE
SHAKES   COFFEE
FLOATS

(BROWN COW   SEASONAL GREENMARKET
(PURPLE COW   SPECIAL PER DAY
              (i.e. SWEET CORN
                 PLUM
                 RASPBERRY)

CHOCOLATE FUDGE COOKIES

HOMEMADE TOPPINGS/MIX-INS
   CHOCOLATE CHUNKS
   HOT CHOCOLATE FUDGE SAUCE
   BUTTERSCOTCH
* SEASONAL   (i.e. BLACK RASPBERRIES
  GREENMARKET   STRAWBERRIES
                    PEACHES
                    APRICOTS
                    GRAPES)
   HOMEMADE PEANUT BUTTER
   CHOCOLATE COOKIES
   WHIPPED CREAM

ESPRESSO/CAPPUCCINO/DRIP COFFEE (ICED)
ICED TEA   —LEMON/SUGAR/SIMPLE SYRUP
HOT CHOCOLATE (SEASONAL)/CHOCOLATE MILK
FRESH OJ/PINEAPPLE JUICE
MILK
WATER
LEMONADE
COKE/ROOT BEER/ 7-UP/GRAPE

DONUTS - 2-3 VARIETIES

10 ½ btls wine
2 BEERS ON TAP - PROPRIETARY

In 2003, Danny sketched his ideas for a permanent kiosk in the Park on the back of a piece of stationery. The eventual Shack is startlingly close to that vision.

Danny's American Roots

Steak 'n Shake

St. Louis, MO Much about this 1934, Midwest-born burger chain inspired Shake Shack. Its motto, "In Sight It Must Be Right," dances around the building like the Shack's menu, and refers to its quality beef as well as its transparency to customers.

Fitz's

St. Louis, MO One of Danny's teenage faves, Fitz's has since closed and reopened, still offering burgers and draft root beer using its original recipe of natural roots, bark, and spices.

Ted Drewes

St. Louis, MO A St. Louis icon since 1936, Ted Drewes pretty much invented the frozen custard Concrete, so-called because it's so thick you can turn it upside down.

Favorites of Richard Coraine

Crown Candy Kitchen

St. Louis, MO This classic soda fountain opened in 1913, specializing in BLTs, milk shakes and malts. Crown continues to draw legions of fans and is a favorite of Danny's.

Pie 'n Burger

Pasadena, CA Since 1963, this California classic has made the kind of flattop griddle burgers Shake Shack loves, from fresh, quality beef and a signature sauce.

The Apple Pan

Los Angeles, CA Made to order and griddled. *LA Times* food critic Jonathan Gold calls the Apple Pan burger (made since 1947) "one of LA's greatest culinary legacies."

on the Upper West Side that we opened in 2008 is a huge part of this story, because not only had we never done anything for a second time, but if that one had not succeeded, there would be no Shake Shack as we know it.

Devouring a ShackBurger at Citi Field.

What can you do about the line? People may not realize the line is a result of cooking everything to order. At MSP there was nothing we could do about the line except open a second restaurant. And maybe I was the first restaurateur in history to be rooting for a little cannibalization. But it didn't happen. When we opened on the Upper West Side, the line only got longer at the first Shack.

Places that make you happy. Shake Shack was emotional from the start. We were flirting with ideas like, wouldn't it be fun to put Shake Shack at the top of a great ski mountain? Citi Field was Shake Shack 2.5. Our question at the Mets game was, did Shake Shack have the power to make you happy even if you were sad about the score? People were coming to the game up to two hours early to get in line at the Shack. That proved to us that people wanted to gather at a Shake Shack no matter where it is.

A learning experience. With every single Shake Shack we opened in those days, we were trying to learn something, asking ourselves, what did we discover about Shake Shack that we never knew before? We wondered if the first one worked only because it was a freestanding building in a park. So, the first few Shake Shacks we opened were adjacent to green space—Upper West Side was across from the park at the Museum of Natural History; Upper East Side had that outdoor patio area (which was constantly under scaffolding).

A mirror of its community. I'll never forget my feeling of joy when I visited the Shacks in Dubai and Kuwait. Seeing the exact same tray of food we served in New York carried by women in burqas, and those women photographing their food and posting on social media, just as folks did at home. Each Shack became a mirror of its place, because there's nothing particularly imposing about the menu. No one has never heard of a hamburger.

When Danny Met Randy

Here's how Danny Meyer remembers it: "One of the single best decisions I ever made was one day in 1999, I picked up a call from a restaurant owner from Seattle, who said, 'You don't know me but there's a young guy, I know him really, really well. Just hire him.' Turns out it was Chris Canlis, whose family owns Canlis, one of the best restaurants in Seattle. And Randy Garutti, who was general manager of Canlis, was the guy he wanted me to meet. That was about the most important job interview I ever had.

"Randy came to work for USHG as our youngest general manager. He was probably about 18! (Really 24!) He became general manager at two of our restaurants, Tabla (2000) and then Union Square Cafe (2003), and then (in 2004) he became Director of Operations for all of our fine dining restaurants which by then included Shake Shack. In 2007, just before we opened our momentous second Shack, we made him Chief Operating Officer. By the end of 2011, Randy became CEO of Shake Shack, and we've never looked back."

In the Beginning ...

"I just felt this big gravitational pull of this little thing in the park and all of its needs, and I just couldn't let it go."

—RICHARD CORAINE, CHIEF DEVELOPMENT OFFICER, USHG

Road warrior Coraine, researching frozen custard at Ted Drewes in St. Louis, 2003.

Richard Coraine has a deep background in fine dining restaurant management and has been with Union Square Hospitality Group since 1996. Less known about RC is that in 2004, *while he was COO of USHG,* he became so obsessed with cooking burgers at the first Shack that his oldest friends didn't hear from him for months; that he cooked in, for luck, the same greasy blue windbreaker; that he staffed the first Shack with ten kids from the then-worst high school in New York.

Many cultural myths surround the birth of Shake Shack, but RC takes it back to 1997,

and a pivotal meeting with MetLife, who owned the building that would house the USHG restaurants Eleven Madison Park and Tabla: "The Met Life people asked us what we envisioned. Danny said, 'Before we get to restaurants, I need to know your plan to develop Madison Square Park.' This was the first meeting I'd ever attended with Danny and it immediately struck me that the park mattered more to him than any restaurant we'd do. The MetLife team had the right answer: 'We plan to raise millions to redevelop that park, because we realize that's as important as anything.' 'I want to be part of that initiative,' Danny said. He told them we would not put restaurants here unless they faced, and (I remember him saying) 'a world class park.' His strategy was 'if we could be part of the improvement of the neighborhood, be a leader on fundraising for the park, then maybe we could get the kiosk.' He already had that idea!"

Whatever we do in the park must satisfy three things, Danny said. "It has to be a magnet for the community, bringing people to the park. Any funds we earn must enrich the park. And it has to be fast, because people who come won't stay long."

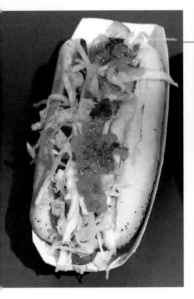

The original Shack team, right; then—Eleven Madison Park chef Kerry Heffernan and pastry chef Nicole Kaplan, 2004. First Chicago dog, neon relish, left.

Let's talk frozen custard. "Danny sent me to find the best frozen custard in America. It had to be as good as Ted Drewes in St. Louis. I flew to St. Louis and went to Ted Drewes every day and stood in the parking lot, sketching their production. Then I set out across the country."

"Our burger has to be great." "Danny's big on benchmarking. To figure out our burger, Danny sent me to Steak 'n Shake in the Midwest. 'I want you to look at how they smash it, hold it down, flip it over and hold it down again.' Our burger became the composite of many places: In-N-Out, where they make everything by hand and to order. I didn't want to do their burger, but I studied their efficiency. Apple Pan's made-to-order griddled burger that's a favorite in LA. Danny was clear, it had to be made on a griddle. You can't get that Steak 'n Shake mashed-down-on-hot-metal crust—on a grill. I've probably eaten 500 times at Pie 'N Burger in Pasadena, and in LA, Mo' Better Meaty Meat Burger."

My pivotal Shake Shack moment: "People kept saying: 'You're the COO of the company. Why are you out there making burgers?' Randy was then my ops guy, my number two, doing all my work. We had his annual review at Eleven Madison Park and suddenly it came to me! I pointed to the Shack: 'Why don't you take that thing in the park and do something with it?' He thought about it for about five seconds and said, 'If you'll give me autonomy, if you'll let me have that as my business, I'll do it.' And I said 'Yes.'"

He's the guy who really had a vision. "Everything that exists today is Randy's doing. He started showing up for meetings in his Shake Shack shirt smelling like burgers. Me? I went back on the road to find the next chef for Eleven Madison Park—Daniel Humm."

Shake Shack - Madison Square Park NYC.

Drawing by James Wines

A Kiosk in the Park

"We designed the Shack as a humorous commentary on commercial architecture, based on the unexpected juxtaposition of pop culture in a historic park."

—JAMES WINES, FOUNDER, SITE

A bit '50s roadside burger stand, a little bit menu-as-building sculpture, and a little bit rock and roll, the original Shack in the park was designed by James Wines and his architectural firm, SITE, famous for Wines' imaginative fusing of art, architecture, and the environment. The designers spent weeks in that park to find their iconic solution, one that reflects the gray tone-on-tone patterns of the nearby Flatiron building. The resulting 20' × 20' building was the Shack heard 'round the world.

Denise MC Lee and her design partner, Sara Stracey, who met at SITE, went on to found Studio SSMC, and to design dozens more Shacks with a wide range of architectural distinction such as Boca Raton, Florida; Westbury, New York; and Austin's Domain. "The original Shack created its own archetype," says Denise. "We discovered how many different ways we could spin it around the world."

Paula Scher, Pentagram
"I love that it worked! I love that they kept with it."

They met in the Park: Pentagram's famed graphic designer, Paula Scher, whose Fifth Avenue offices overlook it, and Danny Meyer, a Park board member, whose little kiosk was about to open. Debbie Landau, then head of the Madison Square Park Conservancy, wanted to ensure that the new kiosk graphics would work with the Paula-designed Park graphics.

"When I looked at that building by SITE, just dropped into the Park, I thought 'moderne,' and 'streamlined.' That's why I chose the Neutra font for the Shake Shack logo. There was this beautiful metal beam that protruded from the building all around which became the perfect place to house the menu type."

Four years later, before the second Shack opened on the Upper West Side, Danny, with Randy, returned to Paula to rethink the graphics. "We developed other takes on the graphic identity, some of which are pretty funny *(see chart),*" Scher says. "But the really wise decision was to keep the Neutra logo. It was already recognized. The Shake Shack logo, the neon burger, and the script type became an easily recognized kit of parts that can and have been used in so many ways."

The Opening Design
The red line through meant NOT your ordinary . . .

Other Ideas
Then we made lots of cow patterns in pretty colors.

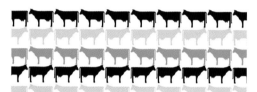

The cows become playful, with food inside—a cow joke.

We tried one where everything shakes and dances.

Today!
The Neutra and the neon, the winning combination.

@whitneytravels

HOW SOCIAL MEDIA SHAPED US

"Shake Shack has an almost McLuhan-esque grasp of media."

—**JOSH OZERSKY**, *Esquire*

"Most restaurants," Ozersky explained, "when their small, cramped quarters can't make enough food to feed their customers, register it as a disaster, issuing public apologies. . . . Shake Shack makes it part of their platform. That huge line of people snaking down the park . . . ? They're having a good time! The line is part of the Shake Shack experience!"

Randy has his own take on social media: "We understand that everything you do you have to share, now. And what does that mean? It forces you to make really good decisions and align yourself with brands whose ethos you share. One of the reasons we're here is that people are proud to share Shake Shack. The iPhone came out in 2007, just before we opened our second Shack. Today, we have hundreds of thousands of followers on Instagram, people proud to post on Facebook and Twitter and Snapchat. You have to share pictures you're proud of. What that means is you might even decide to go to Shake Shack because you know you want to share. Sure, it's your desire to have great food, but it's also your desire to be seen having that food with the people in your life who matter. Social media has intensified our need to be associated with the brands we love."

Illustration by Peter Arkle

Chapter

2

Burger
Bliss

A Short History of the
American Burger

Anyone claiming mastery of the American origin of ground beef on a bun is full of, well, hamburger helper. Choose your favorite creation myth: Did the famed Delmonico's in Lower Manhattan serve America's first "hamburger steak" in 1837? Or, was it at a county fair in 1884 in Seymour, Wisconsin, that Charles Nagreen slapped ground beef between bread? Or did Louis Lasson, as he claims, invent the sandwich in 1900 when he applied toast to ground steak at the still-open Louis' Lunch in New Haven, Connecticut? And what about the good folks of Athens, Texas, who still celebrate Uncle Fletch Hamburger Festival, named for Fletcher Davis, who brought burgers to the 1904 St. Louis World's Fair? We'll never know. . . . But we do know we didn't invent the burger and won't be the last people to make a great one!

MID-1800s
Is it from Hamburg?

True that a "Hamburg steak" was served in restaurants the mid-1800s, feeding travelers crowding ships bound for America from one of the busiest ports in Europe. Its name may come from the German city, but the burger's heart is pure red, white, and blue.

1921
White Castle

Burgers had an image problem in the early 20th century, one that White Castle, America's first fast food restaurant chain, was born to combat. As its founder, Edgar Waldo "Billy" Ingram wrote, "The word 'hamburger' evokes 'dirty, dingy, ill-lighted hole in the wall'" places that serve meat of questionable provenance. With its signature square thin burgers, systematized production, and pristine white porcelain exteriors, White Castle was, by contrast, a clean, well-lighted place, perfect for post–World War I optimism. Ingram opened first in Wichita, KS, partnering with a fry cook named Walter Anderson, and went on to launch more than 400 stores.

1934
Wimpy's

Pop culture met the burger in the personage of J. Wellington Wimpy of Popeye fame whose motto, "I would gladly pay you Tuesday for a hamburger today," became a national catchphrase. Launched in Bloomington, IN, by 1954, Wimpy Grilles had sold over 75 million big burgers and expanded to the United Kingdom.

> *"One of the things that defines us as Americans is our ability to recognize the hamburger as a bundle of meaning, not just a bundle of meat."*
>
> **—JOSH OZERSKY**, *The Hamburger*, 2008

1937

Bob's Big Boy

When Bob Wian created a double-decker, two-patty burger at Bob's Big Boy in Glendale, CA, he launched the burger's cartoon iconography, including, eventually, a 12-foot Big Boy statue. That logo quickly went viral under different names, projecting Big Boy's vibrant roadside personality.

1940

McDonald's

Burgers were forever merged with car culture by two former truck drivers, the brothers Richard and Maurice "Mac" McDonald, who, after failing at running a local movie theater, created a nifty octagonal drive-in burger joint in 1940, in San Bernardino, CA. Burgers cost 15¢. Operational efficiency mattered: it was all about assembly line production, interchangeable employees, and speed. Crowds went wild. By the mid-1950s, when Ray Kroc famously entered the picture, Richard McDonald had designed the Golden Arches model and the brothers had sold some 21 franchises. A restless entrepreneur, owner of a Chicago milkshake mixer company, Kroc is credited with the vision that made McDonald's today's worldwide fast food franchise behemoth.

1948

In-N-Out

If California claims the roots of McDonald's, In-N-Out Burger holds its heart. Launched by Harry and Esther Snyder in Baldwin Park, near Los Angeles, the Snyders embodied brand integrity. In-N-Out never franchised, use quality ingredients, and value their workers—attitudes reinforced by the chain's crisp and clean red, yellow, and white color palette.

2001

The Gourmet Burger

When, in 2001, the French chef Daniel Boulud made a burger as tall as it is wide—of short ribs slow-braised in red wine, wrapped in sirloin, and stuffed with foie gras and black truffles—and served it on a Parmesan bun for $27 at his theater district db Bistro Moderne, his act of decadence or defiance or both rocked the food world. The db Burger (now $35), spawned a frenzy of luxury burgers that hasn't quit. Rare is the chef who does not roll out a mile-high virtuoso stack of dry-aged, grass-fed, haute cuisine cred.

> *"We search for and partner with beef suppliers who meet our standards—we only use beef raised with no added hormones or antibiotics."*
>
> **—JEFFREY AMOSCATO, VP, SUPPLY CHAIN & MENU INNOVATION**

Meat for our burgers comes from Angus cattle that have a pretty idyllic life, grazing as they do on grassy stretches of pastureland in Northern Colorado, above and opposite. That Rocky Mountain scenery just has to impact the flavor. Jeffrey, in Ireland, right.

Sourcing Premium Beef

For a company built on burgers, beef quality is at the core of Shake Shack's belief system. Angus cattle are prized for their muscle meat, and there's no more crucial task than establishing a solid relationship with farmers to ensure the constant supply of "never-ever"—beef raised with no hormones or antibiotics. Like so many Shack leaders, Jeffrey Amoscato, left, has a culinary degree; he was a cook (Jean-Georges, Le Cirque) who became a manager (The Modern), then ran purchasing for USHG before leading our menu and sourcing efforts.

Jeff is charged with assuring quality and consistency of ingredients at home and abroad. "It was trial and error," he recalls. "We took the time to inspect dozens of raw material suppliers and countless processing plants to really understand what our beef patty is today."

"The Shack Secret Blend Dies with Me!"

Meatmaster Pat LaFrieda's swears never to divulge our formula, but the blends he suggests make perfect burgers at home.

Pat LaFrieda, third-generation New York butcher and meat supplier to many of the city's best restaurants, helped us create a proprietary burger blend for the first Shake Shack based on a superior grind of whole muscles, worlds away from the inferior combination of trimmings and added fat in most burger mixes. "I began working with USHG when Floyd Cardoz, then chef at Tabla, suggested I consult with Michael Romano, then chef at Union Square Cafe, on a burger blend," LaFrieda recalls. "But Shake Shack was different from the start."

"I have a passion for logistics," he recalls. "I knew the meat was going from refrigeration at Eleven Madison Park restaurant across the street to a flattop griddle outside in the park—variables that I had not encountered before. So I started worrying about the cooking surface, and how much heat the meat would

Lighter Blend (Think Pinot Noir)

BRISKET　　　　　CHUCK

Mix 25% brisket with 75% chuck for a milder burger.

Richer Blend (Think Cabernet)

SHORT RIB + **CHUCK** =

Mix 20% short rib with 80% chuck for a beefier burger.

lose each time it crossed Park Avenue, and how long it would take to get a sear on the griddle. I knew we needed to create a blend to match those conditions. I think that makes us very different, because most butchers don't even worry about how their meat will be cooked."

Getting it right. Carla Lalli Music, the Shack's 2005 general manager, recalls what it took: "Because we cooked so many of the same burgers daily, changes to the ratio of fat to lean would be obvious immediately. I can remember days in the beginning when the patties shrank too much and gave off a lot of fat, and others when they were too lean and lacked that signature juiciness. We would get on the phone to Pat and report our findings; he'd retool on his end, even sending a new batch that same day, and before too long we were at a place where the burgers hit that sweet spot 999 times out of 1,000."

Freshly ground, never frozen. It almost goes without saying that LaFrieda's meat is ground in the wee hours and delivered fresh to every Shack the next morning. These days, Pat still serves most East Coast Shacks, but he's been part of the family and helps numerous other talented butchers around the globe to match his process.

Making "pucks." "We had never made formed burgers in our history, we just delivered ground meat in a bag," Pat explains. "But Shake Shack asked us to make 'pucks,' which are four ounces of meat in a ball they'd press down on the griddle

CHEF COLLAB

Mark worked with Chef Zaiyu Hasegawa of restaurant Jimbocho DEN in Tokyo to create the DEN Shack, a burger topped with applewood-smoked bacon, red miso Shack-Sauce, sancho peppercorns, and Japanese-style marinated cucumbers.

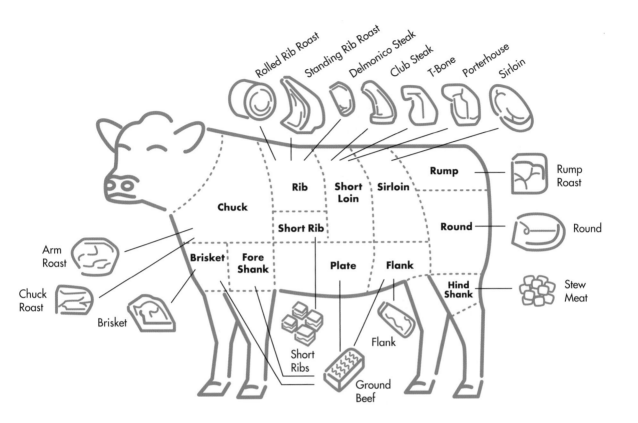

Illustration by Cathie Urushibata.

"If you follow the golden rules that I've laid out for you, you can make your own version of Shake Shack burgers at home. Forget about the economy cuts, the flavor's in the whole muscles."

—PAT LAFRIEDA

to get that famous sear. They told us whatever it cost for labor, they'd understand. So I bought biscuit cutters! We were still working out of Manhattan's meat market, on Pat LaFrieda Lane off Washington Street. And I had a crew of five who did nothing but form burgers all afternoon. That was just for the first Shack in the Park. Eventually, of course, we realized we had to buy machinery to shape our burgers. And that made the process, and the puck even better."

Grinding Your Own (at home!)

Really cold meat's the secret; chill to below freezing first.

Pro Tip

Cutting the meat into smaller pieces before you start makes it easier to feed it into the grinder.

BRISKET

CHUCK

SHORT RIB

The First Grind

Think of this as a rough chop, not a grind, so use the coarser plate first. You'll immediately see a separation: little bits of fat and little bits of protein.

The Second Grind

Grinding the chopped meat again with a finer plate ensures that you get a great mix of both kinds of muscle meat and fat in every bite of your burger.

POTATO BUN

Did you ever think of the ratio of bun to meat? The perfect potato bun never tries to take anything away from the burger: it absorbs juices and cradles the meat. It just does its job beautifully.

UNSALTED BUTTER

Toasting the bun is the way we get a contrast of textures; butter is the secret to crispiness. We say a well toasted bun should look like perfectly cooked French toast.

GREEN LEAF LETTUCE

The ShackBurger is not just about the flavors, it's an extremely visual burger, designed to delight. Frilly green leaf lettuce is more than a refreshing note that offers great textures. Green leaf lettuce is the smile.

OUR SALT & PEPPER MIX

We mix ½ cup kosher salt with ½ teaspoon freshly ground pepper and use that mixture to season our burgers as they cook. You'll see we call for a pinch or two of the mixture in every recipe.

> *"The cheeseburger is a thoroughly contemporary American phenomenon, but it is primal in its capacity to evoke a collective—and positive—human experience."*
>
> **—ELISABETH ROZIN**, *The Primal Cheeseburger*, 1994

ShackBurger

(close enough) ←

SHACKSAUCE

We're surely not going to publish THE formula for our secret sauce. (We're not crazy!) But this recipe *(page 49)* comes pretty darn close with home ingredients. It's our homage to everything sweet, salty, sour, and smoky that's ever been put on top of a burger.

ROMA TOMATOES

Our field-ripened tomatoes are Romas. They are firm enough to hold their shape and color and add a sweet note to balance the salty crust of the burger.

AMERICAN CHEESE

We get ours from Wisconsin, the very heart of American cheese country. It is quite simply the creamiest, meltingest cheese there is, bringing its special tang to a cheeseburger. Buy it sliced: it's easier to drape on a hot burger.

GROUND BEEF

Our burgers are made from our own special blend of freshly ground, all-natural Angus beef, raised with no hormones or antibiotics. It's so flavorful, all you need to season it is salt and pepper.

 45 SECONDS: THE AMOUNT OF TIME IT TAKES FOR THE CHEESE TO MELT.

LOCAL HERO

Martin's Potato Rolls

CHAMBERSBURG, PA

Martin's is an American family story that began in 1955 in Lois and Lloyd Martin's humble kitchen in the heart of Pennsylvania Dutch country. "Mother had a recipe, Dad had a vision," recalls son Jim Martin, now president of the company that turns out tens of millions of potato rolls a week.

Loading his '54 Dodge Coronet with the rolls Lois baked, Lloyd would head to the farmers' market and sell out so fast that he soon converted their one-car garage into a bakery. Now there are two factories, but the rolls are still old-fashioned, made from potatoes, milk, high-protein wheat flour, sunflower oil, sugar, and yeast, and proudly non-GMO. Their signature pale yellow color, once artificial, today comes from turmeric and annatto.

Toast the Buns Ahead

Think of this as a lovely ritual: Heat up your griddle and lavish attention on those buns so they'll be ready the second your burger's done. Begin by melting butter in a small pot. With a soft brush, paint the butter on the insides of the buns. Place butter-side down on the griddle till they're beautifully browned.

Making a ShackBurger *(at home!)*

Great beef, sturdy tools, a bit of practice—and you're in the burger business.

The Right Tools

Stainless steel spatulas are your great friends, above. Sturdiness counts. And for griddles, we love Lodge cast iron, still made by an American company founded in 1896 in South Pittsburg, Tennessee. The cooking surface only improves with use.

Pro Tip

Grease and smoke are inevitable by-products of cooking burgers right. At home we use a large upside down mesh strainer to keep the grease splatter down.

1. The ground beef puck meets the hot griddle pan, seasoned side down.

4. When the edges beneath the burger become dark brown and crisp, and pockets of juices on the surface are bubbling hot, use one of the sturdy spatulas to scrape the burger and its crispy browned crust from the griddle. Another spatula is useful to keep the burger from sliding away.

Push hard! Our grill teams have great forearms.

2. A large, sturdy metal spatula helps firmly smash the ground meat puck into a thick round patty, about 4½ inches wide and ⅓ inch thick.

The first 30 seconds are crucial: that's when you smash the meat to make the most evenly browned burger. Firmly press down on the spatula with another stiff spatula to help flatten the burger quickly.

3. Add 2 pinches of salt and freshly ground pepper to the burger top.

6. Just after the burger is flipped, add the cheese.

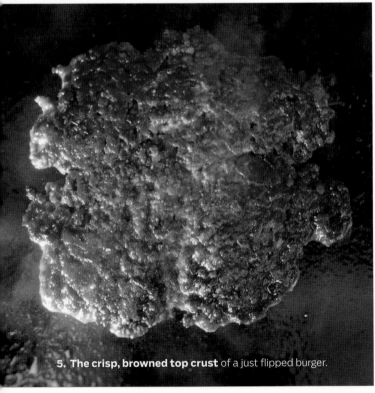

5. The crisp, browned top crust of a just flipped burger.

The ShackBurger

Okay, here's our sacred cow!

MAKES 4

Most likely the reason you have this book in your hands—our version of the great American cheeseburger. Like all deceptively simple things, it took us years to get it right, but now you can master burger perfection in five minutes.

4 **hamburger potato buns**

4 **tablespoons unsalted butter, melted**

4 **tablespoons ShackSauce** *(recipe follows)*

4 **pieces green leaf lettuce**

8 **¼-inch slices ripe plum tomato**

1 **pound very cold ground beef, divided into 4 pucks**

½ **teaspoon Our Salt & Pepper Mix** *(page 40)*

4 **slices American cheese**

1. Heat a cast-iron griddle over medium-low heat until warm. Meanwhile, open the hamburger buns and brush the insides with the melted butter. A soft brush is helpful here. Place the buns buttered side down on the griddle and toast until golden brown, 2 to 3 minutes. Transfer buns to a plate. Spoon the sauce onto the top bun. Add a piece of the lettuce and two slices of tomato.

2. Increase the heat to medium and heat the griddle until hot, 2 to 3 minutes.

3. Evenly sprinkle a pinch of Our Salt & Pepper Mix on top of each puck of meat.

4. Place the pucks on the griddle, seasoned side down. Using a large, sturdy metal spatula, firmly smash each puck into a ⅓-inch-thick round patty. Pressing down on the spatula with another stiff spatula helps flatten the burger quickly. Evenly sprinkle another big pinch of Our Salt & Pepper Mix.

5. Cook the burgers, resisting the urge to move them, until the edges beneath are brown and crisp, and juices on the surface are bubbling hot, about 2½ minutes. Slide one of the spatulas beneath the burger to release it from the griddle and scrape up the caramelized browned crust. Use the other spatula to steady the burger and keep it from sliding. Flip the burgers. Put the cheese on top and cook the burgers 1 minute longer for medium. Cook more or less depending on your preference.

6. Transfer the cheeseburgers to the prepared buns and enjoy.

ShackSauce *(close enough)*

MAKES ABOUT ½ CUP

Long ago we threw away the key to the secret recipe for ShackSauce; but we promise to get you really close with ingredients easily found in your kitchen.

½ **cup Hellmann's mayonnaise**	¼ **teaspoon kosher dill pickling brine**
1 **tablespoon Dijon mustard**	**Pinch of cayenne pepper**
¾ **teaspoon Heinz ketchup**	

Put all the ingredients in a small mixing bowl and stir until well combined. Sauce will keep, covered, in the refrigerator for up to one week.

LOCAL HERO

Lucky Lee Tomatoes

CENTRAL FLORIDA

You can't make this stuff up! Lucky Lee, whose real name is Karen, was part of a performing family group called The Sunrise Show Band, when their Florida grandmother fell ill. The family left show business and moved to Ruskin, in central Florida, where they discovered the tomato business. "What if we brought a truckload of fresh, juicy, field-grown, vine-ripened tomatoes to New York in the dead of winter?" they thought. Lucky visited restaurant kitchens with "a box on my shoulder and a knife in my belt," cajoling chefs to sample. Lucky Lee's tomatoes are worlds away from the dubious practices of factory farms portrayed in Barry Estabrook's *Tomatoland*. "Ours is a craft business; we only pick when ripe," says Lee, chief supplier of Roma tomatoes to many New York Shake Shacks.

SmokeShack

Peanut Butter Bacon Burger

Smoke Shack

MAKES 4

Here's our version of a burger based on everything that's great about smoky bacon. For this recipe, Mark went deep into his Italian-American childhood, remembering his mother's pan-fried pork chops with cherry peppers, and how the spicy pickled peppers balanced the richness of the pork.

4 **hamburger potato buns, toasted** *(page 42)*	½ **teaspoon Our Salt & Pepper Mix** *(page 40)*
4 **tablespoons unsalted butter, melted**	4 **slices American cheese**
4 **tablespoons ShackSauce** *(page 49)*	8 **slices double-smoked bacon, cooked, broken in half** *(page 54)*
1 **pound very cold ground beef, divided into 4 pucks**	8 **tablespoons diced pickled red cherry peppers**

Follow the ShackBurger recipe on page 48, topping the cheeseburger with great bacon (we love Niman Ranch, *page 55*) and red cherry peppers instead of lettuce and tomato.

Peanut Butter Bacon Burger

MAKES 4

Among devoted Shack fans, this burger has cult status. It's only officially been served twice in our history! But folks know they can always order a bacon hamburger and ask us for a side of peanut butter sauce.

4 **hamburger potato buns, toasted** *(page 42)*	8 **slices cooked bacon, broken in half** *(page 54)*
4 **tablespoons unsalted butter, melted**	8 **tablespoons smooth peanut butter, thinned with a little canola oil**
1 **pound very cold ground beef, divided into 4 pucks**	
½ **teaspoon Our Salt & Pepper Mix** *(page 40)*	

Follow the ShackBurger recipe on page 48, topping the burger with great bacon and two spoonfuls of thinned peanut butter instead of lettuce, tomato, cheese, and ShackSauce.

Think Like a Burger Maker

By Mark Rosati

My favorite burger is a plain cheeseburger. I wish it were more complicated, but it's not. If the meat is fresh (say "No" to that convenient packaged pre-ground meat, and just once, have whole muscles ground for you; I promise, you'll taste the difference), well seasoned (simply, with salt and freshly ground pepper), properly cooked with a nice salty crust (a quick sear on a hot, flat surface to lock in the juices, but not cooked so long those juices dry up), the cheese is melted and creamy, and its cradled by a bun that's nicely toasted yet still soft and pillowy on the outside, I don't ask for anything more.

That is the most perfect burger bite of my life: when the interior juices of the burger meet the creaminess of the cheese, comingle, and create a natural sauce. If you understand the basics, you can have that experience, too. It's the most primal, simple, and pleasurable expression of what a great burger is all about.

Cooking Bacon

MAKES 8 SLICES

Preheat the oven to 375°F. Lay 8 slices of bacon on a parchment paper–lined baking pan. Bake until the bacon is browned and crisp, about 15 minutes. Transfer the bacon to a paper towel–lined plate to drain. Break in half to top burgers.

Pro Tip: After it's been cooked, Mark likes to dice the bacon into small pieces and sprinkle it on top of cheese fries and especially over cheese dogs—his favorite.

LOCAL HERO

Niman Ranch Bacon

MIDWEST, USA

As Mark Rosati says "the texture of Niman's bacon is so soft and juicy. That, coupled with their cure and smoke levels, produces one of the most flavor bacons I've ever tasted, which, of course, highlights the quality of their amazing pork."

Not by accident. Niman Ranch is an association of about 800 farmers, like Paul Willis, above, all from family-owned and operated farms, mostly in the Midwest.

Niman is advised by the famed Dr. Temple Grandin, the animal expert whose sustainable practices have made Niman's animal and land management protocols even more humane. Bacon is minimally processed with no artificial ingredients; it's smoked four days over applewood, in a smokehouse that's been in continuous production for over 100 years. We use Niman in our Shacks; substitute quality bacon such as D'Artagnan.

"We love hand crafting each Shack, infusing it with locally inspired flavors."

—MARK ROSATI

Lockhart Link

South Texas born & bred

Lockhart Link

MAKES 4

This burger was created for the opening of our first Austin Shack to celebrate everything that's great about Texas barbecue, especially the smoked jalapeño cheese sausage made by Kreuz Market in Lockhart, Texas, an hour south. You can order the very same sausage at kreuzmarket.com or use your favorite smoked sausage links.

- **4** hamburger potato buns, toasted *(page 42)*
- **4** tablespoons unsalted butter, melted
- **4** tablespoons ShackSauce *(page 49)*
- **8** slices round kosher dill pickle
- **2** 3-ounce smoked jalapeño cheese sausage links, halved lengthwise
- **1** pound very cold ground beef, divided into 4 pucks
- **½** teaspoon Our Salt & Pepper Mix *(page 40)*
- **4** slices American cheese

1. Follow the ShackBurger recipe on page 48, topping the burger with pickles and a griddled sausage (we love Kreuz Market's) instead of lettuce and tomato.

2. For the sausages: Heat the griddle over medium heat until hot, 2 to 3 minutes. Put the sausages on the griddle cut side down and cook until golden brown and crisp, about 2 minutes. Flip the sausages and cook about 2 minutes more. We like to cook the sausages ahead and keep them warm in the oven while we make the burgers.

Kreuz Jalapeño Cheese Sausage

LOCKHART, TX

The entire town of Lockhart, Texas, is redolent of the fragrant wood smoke that has given the place its livelihood ever since Charles Kreuz started smoking meats out of his grocery here in 1900. The jalapeño cheese sausages we serve in some of our Texas Shacks are pre-smoked for about two hours, then finished over Texas split post oak wood. As Emmylou Harris sings, "If I could only win your love . . ." Kreuz Market's smokehouse turns out about 2,400 sausage rings a day: "85 percent beef, 15 percent pork, 100 percent truth," spiced with black pepper, salt, and cayenne in natural casings. *Texas Monthly* calls Kreuz sausage "truly one of the best in Barbecueland."

ShackMeister Burger

MAKES 4

Where do our burger ideas come from? This one was born to compete at the annual Burger Bash at the South Beach Wine & Food Festival in Miami. Not surprisingly, every one of us had an opinion. Ultimately, good old-fashioned comfort and simplicity triumphed. We went with our simplest burger. And we won!

4	hamburger potato buns, toasted *(page 42)*
4	tablespoons unsalted butter, melted
4	tablespoons ShackSauce *(page 49)*

1	pound very cold ground beef, divided into 4 pucks
½	teaspoon Our Salt & Pepper Mix *(page 40)*
4	slices American cheese
4	ounces ShackMeister Fried Shallots

Follow the ShackBurger recipe on page 48, topping the burger with the Fried Shallots instead of lettuce and tomato.

ShackMeister Fried Shallots

MAKES ABOUT 1½ CUPS

Okay, we'll be honest: these fried shallots are our version of onion rings. We prefer the garlicky flavor of shallots, and because they're smaller than onions, we can add more delicious crispy bits to our burgers and flat-top dogs! The marinade balances the shallots' sweetness with the slightly bitter edge of beer. Making them is easier than you think.

½	pound shallots, peeled and thinly sliced crosswise
1	teaspoons freshly ground black pepper
1½	cups ShackMeister or other ale

1½	cups flour
	Canola oil for frying
	Salt

1. Put the shallots, ½ teaspoon of the pepper, and ale into a bowl. Cover and marinate in the refrigerator for at least 12 hours and up to 24 hours.

2. Mix together the remaining ½ teaspoon pepper with the flour in a wide deep dish. Strain the marinated shallots, discarding the marinade.

3. Pour the oil into a deep pot to a depth of 3 inches. Heat over medium heat until the oil reaches a temperature of 350ºF on a candy thermometer. Meanwhile, working in batches, dredge the shallots in the seasoned flour until evenly coated. Transfer them to a sieve, and shake off excess flour.

4. Working in small batches, deep-fry the shallots in the hot oil, turning them halfway through, until golden and crisp, about 1½ minutes. Transfer them with a slotted spoon to drain on paper towels. Season with salt.

Making ShackMeister Fried Shallots (at home!)

Fried onion rings have nothing on these crispy little beauties.

1. Slice peeled shallots crosswise and into thick rings.

2. Marinate sliced shallots in ale and pepper for 12 to 24 hours, refrigerated.

4. Shake off excess flour using a strainer.

5. Fry shallots in batches in 3 inches of hot oil.

3. Dredge strained marinated shallots and mix well with flour.

6. Drain fried shallots on paper towels and salt well.

• **ShackBurger with ShackMeister Ale.** Burgers don't run scared—they need a slight caramelized sweetness to enhance the char of the meat, ennoble the onions, and wake up the bun. Carbonation is a major ally of the ShackBurger; the "scrubbing bubbles" zap right through the cheese. Pale ales are best; their caramelized malts anchor the pairing while the hops slice through the middle.

• **SmokeShack with Brown Ales.** You'll be surprised how well brown ales work with this burger. The toastiness of roasted malts really grabs on to the smokiness of the bacon.

• **'Shroom Burger with Belgian Ales.** Belgian abbey ales, with their almost-raisiny caramelized flavor, are so good with the earthiness of the 'Shroom Burger. Or, try bourbon barrel-aged beers, particularly porters, with their rich vanilla-like American oakiness. Try "Berliner weisse," or "sour beer," a light, tart beer originally German, but American brewers make them now (and their slightly salty cousin, "Gose").

—*Garrett Oliver, Brooklyn Brewery*

Surf 'N Shack

MAKES 4

Mark grew up in New England with lobster and clam shacks literally in his backyard. So a mashup of burger stands and seafood shacks seemed a natural: surf 'n'turf on a bun. ShackSauce, it turns out, works magic on lobster, too.

4 hamburger potato buns, toasted (page 42)

4 tablespoons unsalted butter, melted

4 pieces green leaf lettuce

8 slices ripe plum tomato, sliced ¼ inch thick

1 pound very cold ground beef, divided into 4 pucks

½ teaspoon Our Salt & Pepper Mix (page 40)

1 recipe Shack Lobster Salad

Follow the ShackBurger recipe on page 48, hold the ShackSauce and cheese, and top that great burger with lobster salad.

Shack Lobster Salad

MAKES ABOUT 1½ CUPS

Steam your own lobsters, if you like, or buy them freshly cooked at a good seafood market.

2 1-pound lobsters, steamed, cooled, meat removed from shell and cut into ½-inch pieces

6 tablespoons ShackSauce (page 49) or Hellman's mayonnaise

2 teaspoons fresh lemon juice

¼ teaspoon celery salt

Salt and pepper

Put lobster meat, ShackSauce, lemon juice, and celery salt into a mixing bowl and gently stir to combine. Season with salt and pepper. Keep cold until ready to serve.

Now that's quite a catch!

Roadside Double

MAKES 4

We created this burger for the opening of our first Shack in Los Angeles (America's burger capitol!) to salute the city's culinary traditions. We loved the region's iconic French Dip where rich au jus enhances the flavor of the beef. Our Bacon and Beer–Simmered Onions add that richness and then some—especially to a double cheeseburger.

4	hamburger potato buns, toasted *(page 42)*
4	tablespoons unsalted butter, melted
8	teaspoons Dijon mustard
2	pounds very cold ground beef, divided into 8 pucks
1	teaspoon Our Salt & Pepper Mix *(page 40)*
8	slices Swiss cheese
1	recipe Bacon and Beer–Simmered Onions, warm

Follow the ShackBurger recipe on page 48, spooning mustard instead of ShackSauce onto the top bun and stacking two cheeseburgers on each bun. Top with a generous helping of Bacon and Beer–Simmered Onions instead of lettuce and tomato.

Bacon and Beer–Simmered Onions

MAKE 1 CUP

Mark was inspired by the old-fashioned griddled onion toppings at roadside burger stands, but he picked up a few modern touches from the British chef Heston Blumenthal, who likes to add star anise to onions for extra richness.

1	teaspoon canola oil
4	slices bacon, cut crosswise into ¼-inch-thick pieces
2	medium onions, peeled, halved lengthwise, and sliced ½ inch thick
1	tablespoon unsalted butter, diced
½	teaspoon kosher salt
½	cup ale
1	teaspoon balsamic vinegar
½	bay leaf
½	star anise

1. Put the oil and bacon in a medium saucepan and cook over medium heat, stirring often, until the bacon is golden brown and crisp, about 5 minutes. Add the onions, butter, and salt and stir until the onions are evenly coated.

2. Cover the pan and cook, stirring often, until the onions are soft and translucent, about 20 minutes.

3. Add the ale, vinegar, bay leaf, and star anise. Cook, uncovered, stirring frequently, until the liquid has almost evaporated and the onions are very soft and caramelized, about 40 minutes. Remove and discard the bay leaf and star anise.

'Shroom Burger

MAKES 4

We knew that our idea of a community gathering place meant we wanted to offer our vegetarian guests more than just fries to munch on. We set out to create a vegetarian experience even meat eaters would crave. Hence the 'Shroom Burger's crispy mushroom halves surrounding a creamy, cheesy filling. After it became so popular, we created the Shack Stack, piling a 'Shroom Burger atop a ShackBurger, so our meat-loving friends can get in on the 'Shroom action.

For the mushroom caps:
- 4   4-inch portabello mushroom caps
- ¼ cup canola oil
- ½ teaspoon kosher salt
- ⅛ teaspoon freshly ground black pepper
- 1½ cups flour
- 3 eggs
- 2 cups panko bread crumbs

For the filling:
- 1½ cups grated muenster
- ½ cup grated cheddar
- ½ teaspoon minced onion
- ⅛ teaspoon minced garlic
- ¼ teaspoon flour
- 1 egg yolk
- 1 pinch cayenne

To cook and assemble the mushroom burgers:
- Canola oil for deep-frying
- Kosher salt
- 4 tablespoons ShackSauce *(page 49)*
- 4 hamburger potato buns, toasted *(page 42)*
- 4 pieces green leaf lettuce
- 8 ¼-inch slices ripe plum tomato

1. For the mushroom caps, preheat the oven to 375°F. Put mushroom caps on a medium baking pan. Rub caps all over with the oil, then season both sides with the salt and pepper. Arrange mushrooms gill side down in a single layer and roast until tender, 30 to 35 minutes. Remove from the oven and set aside to cool. Slice mushrooms in half horizontally.

2. Put the flour in a wide dish, beat the eggs in another wide dish, and put the panko in a third wide dish and set aside.

3. For the filling, mix together the muenster and cheddar cheeses, onion, garlic, flour, egg yolk, and cayenne in a medium mixing bowl. Set aside.

4. Shape the filling into 4 equal disks, ½ inch smaller in diameter than the mushroom caps. Place cheese disks on gill side of each mushroom cap, cover with other half of cap, cut side down, and gently press together to secure the filling.

5. Dredge the stuffed mushroom caps in the flour, then dip in the beaten egg, coating them completely, then dredge in the panko. Set prepared mushrooms on a plate and refrigerate while heating the oil to deep-fry them.

6. To cook the mushroom burgers, pour the oil into a deep, wide pot to a depth of 3 inches. Heat over medium heat until the oil reaches a temperature of 350°F on a candy thermometer. Deep-fry the prepared mushrooms, one or two at a time, until golden brown and crisp all over, about 3 or 4 minutes. Transfer mushrooms with a slotted spoon to drain on paper towels. Season with salt.

7. Spoon the ShackSauce onto the top bun. Add a piece of lettuce and two slices of tomato.

8. Transfer the mushroom burgers to the prepared buns. Enjoy!

Making the 'Shroom Burger

Nice to know the secrets, even if you'd rather have yours at a Shack!

1. Roast portabello mushroom caps rubbed with oil at 375ºF for 30 minutes.

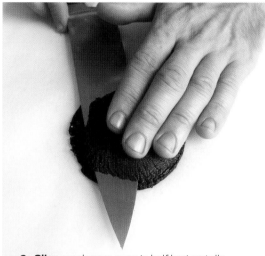

2. Slice mushroom caps in half horizontally.

4. Fill the bottom of the cap with cheese stuffing shaped into a small disk.

5. Coat the stuffed mushrooms with flour, egg, and panko.

3. Separate the two halves of the mushroom caps.

6. Fry stuffed mushrooms one or two at a time in the hot oil.

John Folse

GONZALES, LA

Chef John Folse is famous in Louisiana for his culinary institute, his restaurants, and his weighty cookbooks. But it was his food preparation facilities that became crucial to Shake Shack. Right after 9/11, Folse decided to "adopt" a New York restaurant and chose Eleven Madison Park to lavish weekly Cajun Care Packages of music and food. "I don't think anyone even knew who Chef John Folse was," he recalls. "They came to realize we were just chefs in Louisiana thinking about them. We did what people do to help." After Jeff Amoscato read about Folse's processing facilities, he reached out: "To find one supplier with the ability to make so many different items is rare. Then we connected the dots back to USHG in 2001." Folse likes his version: "The fact that I'm now producing 'Shroom Burgers and ShackSauce didn't happen because I'm a great manufacturer, it happened because we fed a bunch of restaurant folks after 9/11."

Breakfast Shacks

We knew we needed an iconic breakfast sandwich that would deliver an experience as memorable as the ShackBurger. It had to be simple, high quality, and delicious. Now, in select Shacks, we offer breakfast three ways: Egg 'N Cheese, Bacon Egg 'N Cheese, and Sausage Egg 'N Cheese.

Egg 'N Cheese

MAKES 4

4 hamburger potato buns, toasted *(page 42)*	½ teaspoon Our Salt & Pepper Mix *(page 40)*
2 teaspoons butter	4 slices American cheese
4 large eggs	

1. Heat the butter in a large nonstick skillet over medium-low heat. Crack the eggs into the skillet, add a pinch of Our Salt & Pepper Mix, and fry until the whites are opaque and the yolks are beginning to set, 3 to 4 minutes. Gently flip the eggs. Put the cheese on top and fry the eggs until the yolks are no longer runny, 2 to 3 minutes.

2. Transfer each egg to the toasted bun and enjoy.

For the Bacon Egg 'N Cheese: To the Egg 'N Cheese, add 8 slices double-smoked bacon *(page 54)*, broken in half, and top each sandwich with 4 half slices.

For the Sausage Egg 'N Cheese: To the Egg 'N Cheese, add breakfast sausage patties or great, freshly made breakfast sausage.

Breakfast Sausage Patties

MAKES 4 4-INCH PATTIES

1 small clove garlic, peeled and finely minced	1½ teaspoons kosher salt
½ teaspoon finely chopped fresh sage	½ teaspoon Aleppo pepper flakes
1 tablespoon maple sugar	2 pinches freshly ground black pepper
	1 pound ground pork

1. Mix together the seasonings and spices in a medium mixing bowl. Add the pork and gently mix until evenly combined. Cover and refrigerate for at least 2 hours and up to 3 days.

2. When you're ready to cook, gently form the sausage mixture into 4-inch patties.

3. Heat a cast-iron griddle over medium heat until hot, 2 to 3 minutes. Cook the sausage patties until browned and crisp, about 2 minutes. Flip the patties and cook until the second side is well browned, another 2 minutes. Transfer sausage patties to a plate and keep warm.

Notes from the Shack Chef

Mark Rosati's food finesse echoes around the block and around the world.

Even though culinary director Mark Rosati had come to New York to study film in 2002, he found himself talking his way into Tom Colicchio's kitchen at USHG's Gramercy Tavern. "I'd met Tom at a food festival and peppered him with endless questions about how he braised his legendary short ribs. 'Either you're insane, or you're really curious about cooking,' he said, inviting me to trail in his kitchen. I was so clueless about what a trail was, I showed up in a suit and tie!

"I absolutely loved the feel and energy of the kitchen, how the meat roaster used butter and crushed garlic to baste a sirloin steak. I was hooked. I wanted to learn this and all that came with it. I wanted burns and scars. I said 'I'll happily wash your stove, cut your carrots, finely slice your chives,

Below: Upper West Side Shack today. Below right, Randy and Danny flank early Shack leader David Swinghamer. Opposite, Mark in his element.

whatever you need.' Deveining foie gras, pushing bone marrow—as I touched these ingredients, the fever grew. I worked two months for free. 'We can't get rid of you,' they said and hired me as a line cook. In 2006, when the new chef, Michael Anthony, arrived, I was further humbled mastering his all-American, vegetable-centric cooking. Then I thought: Since I love restaurants, I need to learn the front of the house.

"In 2007, the only opening for a manager at USHG was Shake Shack. I was grossly underqualified, and ambivalent about Shake Shack to be honest. I was offered a trail at the Madison Square Park Shack, and saw the quality of their ingredients, how everything was made fresh daily. I saw how their passion for cooking was like a fine dining restaurant's: you don't buy the sauces or the pastry mix-ins, you make them! I saw how jazzed the staff was. It was not 'How're we going to meet budget goals?' but 'How're we going to

cook for 2,000 people, have fun, and make everyone happy today?' Randy, that great cheerleader, convinced them to hire me.

"I'd been offered a job as a server at Per Se, and when I called to turn it down for Shake Shack, the person in charge of hiring said: 'I don't blame you. You'll learn management and hospitality from the best. I'd do it too!' As kitchen manager at MSP, I focused on my culinary strengths: 'Let's sauté those onions longer to build flavor before adding the cream for the cheese sauce.'

"A year later, I helped open the second Shack on the Upper West Side. That was Randy's baby. I couldn't have been more excited. In my mind, I was not opening another Shake Shack, I was opening another Danny Meyer restaurant. It was a huge learning experience: We tore that restaurant down and rebuilt it numerous times, obsessing over lighting, signage, kitchen flow. The night before we opened, Danny

comes in and says, 'Beautiful. But the kitchen is way too bright. I wish the drop down above the counter was a little lower so guests could see the beautiful dining room before the kitchen.' So we call the construction guys in to work all night in our beautiful, clean restaurant. Danny was right, as always. We worked long days, barely sleeping, then talked into the night about how to work more efficiently. I was living on the bun station; Randy was living on expediting. Planning openings at Citi Field and Miami Beach, Randy asked me to focus on crafting new and locally inspired menus."

Fast forward: Today Mark can be as easily found in Minneapolis as London, Tokyo, or the Middle East, making the connection with food and culture. "I'll go to Seoul to meet food people. I know we want to deliver on what they fell in love with at MSP, but we want to reach out into their culture, too, and find local flavors that celebrate where we are."

John Williams

Jonah Beer

Frog's Leap Winery

RUTHERFORD, CA

This was one of Shake Shack's first relationships with growers and producers. Not surprisingly, the Frog's Leap partnership originated with Danny Meyer and the values he shared with owner and winemaker John Williams. Frog's Leap was an early pioneer in dry-farming, making wine with organically grown grapes, caring for the well-being of its workers as well as the soil.

In 2007, with Randy and Frog's Leap's general manager, Jonah Beer, the relationship was cemented. As Beer tells the story,

"They wanted us to make a wine that would fit with Shake Shack's culture, food, and experience. It's quite a jump from thinking alike to making something together.

"If they knew how fast they would grow, they didn't tell us! Shake Shack was very upfront about letting Frog's Leap be the winemaking experts. The custom reds and whites we make exclusively for Shake Shack are fruit forward, with a bright acidity that enlivens their food." Together we created what became Shack Red and Shack White.

Jonah Beer of Frog's Leap Winery pairs our favorites with his favorites.

• **ShackBurger with Cabernet Sauvignon.** When I'm about to tuck into the classic ShackBurger, the fattiness of the beef, the melted cheese, the soft, sweet, potato bun just cry out for a bold Cab. Our custom Shack Red (Cab's a critical component) with its ripe, black fruit flavors (think cassis and currant) beautifully sets off that burger.

• **SmokeShack with Zinfandel.** We need even more fruit to balance the flavors of the Smoke Shack's crisp, salty bacon and slightly sweet cherry peppers. I'd opt for the wild berry razz-ma-tazz of Zinfandel. Its clean fruit flavors play nicely off the smoke and peppers.

• **Peanut Butter Bacon Burger with Shack White.** I'd pair our Sauvignon blanc–based Shack White with this bad boy. The peanut butter brings more salty, creamy goodness to the smoky, salty bacon and pulls out the nuttiness of the burger itself. You need a wine with bright (read: racy) acid. Our Shack White is based on Sauvignon Blanc, a wine defined by and cherished for its acid. With crisp, apple- and pear-like flavors, Shack White works especially well because of the peanut butter . . . like dragging an apple slice through an open jar of PB.

• **'Shroom Burger with Merlot.** With that portobello's savory umami, I'd choose a well-aged red, say 10–15 years. With time in the bottle, reds like Merlot move toward a balanced flavor profile of fruit, earth, and "sous bois," which means forest floor. Those hints of truffle, porcini, and soy in the wine just enhance the burger's richness.

• **Hamburger with Abita Draft Root Beer.** What about those little rug rats you have in tow? Well, this ain't France, so we're not giving them wine! But, that doesn't mean the kids should be left out! When Junior orders a hamburger, suggest he pair it with Abita Draft Root Beer. Hell, pour it in the GoVino wineglass so he can swirl and sip it like the grown-ups! The root beer's loaded with spice and sassafras flavors that highlight the burger's simple goodness. The bubbly, bright fizz tames the sweet, potato bun.

CHEF COLLAB

"We never forget our culinary heritage, so we love teaming up with the world's greatest chefs."

—RANDY GARUTTI

Because Shake Shack was born from a fine dining sensibility, it seems natural for us to reach our to some of our chef friends and others we've long admired to cook up imaginative limited-time treats. We try to capture each chef's unique style and personality within the context of the Shack, and to surprise and delight our mutual fans. Besides the stellar examples here and throughout the book, we've collaborated with Ford Fry in Atlanta, Lee Wolen of BOKA in Chicago, Marc Vetri in Philadelphia, Sat Bains of his Restaurant Sat Bains in Nottingham, UK, and Zaiyu Hasegawa of DEN restaurant in Tokyo and so many others.

Mark carries this quote, attributed to Eleanor Roosevelt, on his phone: "The greatest pursuit of an artist is collaboration. Especially drunken collaboration with friends."

78

Clockwise from above left:
Chef April Bloomfield; team
Eleven Madison Park, Daniel
Humm, Will Guidara, Randy,
and Dustin Wilson. Mark with
David Chang; Danny and
Randy with Dominique Ansel.

Momofuku Shrimp Stack

David Chang *surprises with a shrimp patty and homemade pickles.*

MAKES 4

This is our adaptation of a great collaborative burger we made for our 10th Anniversary. David suspected his fans would expect him to do a pork-topped burger: he wanted to surprise. His idea was to add smoky richness with shrimp patties, then layer on the crunch (pickles), and the umami with his inspired sauce.

4 **hamburger buns, toasted** *(page 42)*	4 **cooked Shrimp Patties**
Momofuku Hozon Sauce	**Cucumber and Red Onion Pickles**
4 **cooked ShackBurger patties** *(page 48)*	4 **leaves bibb lettuce**

To assemble, spread Momofuku Hozon Sauce on both buns. On the bottom bun, layer on the cheeseburger, then the shrimp patty. Top with a few slices of the cucumber and red onion pickles, and a lettuce leaf.

For the Momofuku Hozon Sauce: Combine 4 tablespoons each of Kewpie mayonnaise, ketchup, and miso paste in a small bowl. Mix and set aside.

For the Shrimp Patties: In a food processor fit with a steel blade, combine 1 pound 16–20 count shrimp, shelled and deveined, 1 tablespoon Kochu karu (Korean chili powder), and 1 teaspoon kosher salt. Process until the shrimp has the consistency of loose sausage.

Divide the processed shrimp into 4 equal pucks. Place into an oiled cast-iron pan over medium-high heat, and flatten with a greased spatula. When the bottom turns a slight pink color, flip the patty and cook through, about 2 minutes on each side.

For the Cucumber and Red Onion Pickles: Slice 1 Kirby cucumber into ⅛-inch discs, add 1 tablespoon of sugar and 1 teaspoon salt and combine in a small bowl. In another bowl, combine 1 red onion, peeled and thinly sliced with a tablespoon each of sugar and salt. Let both sit for 10 minutes. Taste and add more sugar or salt if needed. Refrigerate for up to 4 hours.

The Piggie Shack

Daniel Boulud *piles on the barbecue sauce, pulled pork, and slaw.*

MAKES 4

The same year our first hot dog touched down in Madison Square Park, Daniel turned his vaunted culinary prowess into the now-famous db Burger *(page 31)*. With Shake Shack's similar fine dining roots, we were thrilled to kick off our 10-year celebration with this adaptation of his recipe.

4 hamburger buns, toasted *(page 42)*

¼ cup Jalapeño Mayonnaise

8 pieces bibb lettuce

4 cooked ShackBurger patties *(page 48)*

2 cups good quality pulled pork, mixed with ½ cup of your favorite barbecue sauce, warm

Cabbage Vinegar Slaw

4 pickled jalapeños

4 small wooden skewers

To assemble the burgers: Spread Jalapeño Mayonnaise on the bottom and top buns. Add a leaf of lettuce to the bottom bun, then a burger patty, the pulled pork (Daniel like a bourbon-based North Carolina–style mustardy sauce), the cabbage slaw, and more bibb lettuce. Stick a pickled jalapeño on a skewer and into the top bun.

For the Jalapeño Mayonnaise: In a small pan over medium-high heat, add 1 teaspoon of olive oil and sauté 1 small jalapeño pepper, seeded and finely diced, until just cooked, about 3 minutes. Add 2 teaspoons white wine vinegar and reduce completely. Cool the jalapenos in the refrigerator. Daniel would make the mayonnaise, but you can mix ¼ cup of your favorite mayo with the cooled jalapeños in a small bowl.

For the Cabbage Vinegar Slaw: Thinly slice one head red cabbage, toss with salt, and let drain for 3 hours. In a small pot, combine ½ cup apple cider vinegar, ½ cup sugar, ¼ cup mustard, 1 grated garlic clove, and a pinch of salt; bring to a boil. Put the cabbage in a large bowl and pour the hot sauce over it. Chill for at least 3 hours and drain excess liquid before using.

Humm Burger

Daniel Humm *dashed across Park Avenue bearing black truffles.*

MAKES 4

Since we were literally born out of the kitchen at Eleven Madison Park, it was a thrill to serve this truffle-laden burger on Shake Shack's anniversary 10 years later. EMP owner Will Guidara even actually rolled their champagne cart out to the Shack in Madison Square Park to help us celebrate.

4 **hamburger buns, toasted** *(page 42)*

4 **tablespoons Truffle Mayonnaise**

4 **slices Gruyère**

4 **cooked ShackBurger patties** *(page 48)*

8 **strips cooked bacon, broken in half**

1 **medium black truffle (half finely chopped, half shaved)**

Celery Relish

4 **bibb lettuce leaves**

To assemble the Humm Burger, spoon 1 tablespoon truffle mayonnaise on the top of each bun. Put the Gruyère-topped ShackBurger on the bottom, then the bacon, the celery relish, the shaved black truffle and the lettuce.

For the Truffle Mayonnaise: To ¼ cup of your favorite mayonnaise in a small bowl, add a finely chopped half truffle and mix well.

For the Pickled Mustard Seeds: In a saucepan, combine 1 cup white balsamic vinegar, ½ cup sugar, ½ water, and 3 tablespoons kosher salt. Bring to a simmer, stirring to dissolve. Pour the hot pickling liquid into a glass container over ½ cup mustard seeds. Refrigerate overnight.

For the Celery Relish: Bring a pot of salted water to a boil. Prepare an ice bath. Peel and dice small ½ cup celery root and ¼ cup celery. Blanch separately until tender, and shock both in the ice bath. Drain the celeries and combine with ¼ cup half-sour pickles, diced small, 3 tablespoons drained pickled mustard seeds *(above)*, and 1 tablespoon white balsamic vinegar in a medium bowl. Season with salt and set aside.

Cabrito Butter Burger

Andrew Zimmern *wasn't happy till he got his goat.*

MAKES 4

Andrew has always been a huge Shake Shack fan and it was such a treat to work with a chef and charismatic TV personality who loves food and travel so much. What he made was a Midwestern butter burger, featuring his beloved goat.

4   **hamburger buns, toasted** *(page 42)*

20 **ounces ground goat meat divided into 4 patties (recommend 75/25 lean-to-fat ratio)**

Salt and pepper

Seasoned butter

Roasted tomatoes

Roasted onions

Bread and butter pickles

Season the goat patties with salt and pepper. Grill the burgers until medium-rare. Place a dollop of the room-temperature, seasoned butter on the burger to melt just before it's finished cooking. Place the goat patty on the bun, topping with roasted tomatoes and onions. Serve with bread and butter pickles.

For the seasoned butter: Let 1 stick butter come to room temperature. In a stand mixer with a paddle, whip the butter until it is creamed, about 20 seconds. Add 1 tablespoon minced parsley, 1 tablespoon finely minced shallot, 1 tablespoon minced tarragon, ½ teaspoon ground white pepper, 2 tablespoons lemon juice, and ½ teaspoon Colman's dry gound mustard. Scrape down the sides of the mixing bowl and pulse the mixer to evenly distribute the herbs and butter.

For the roasted tomatoes: Preheat the oven to 225ºF. Halve 12 Roma tomatoes. In a mixing bowl, toss with 3 tablespoons olive olive oil to coat, and season with salt and pepper. Place the tomatoes cut-side up on a small baking pan lined with parchment paper. Bake in the upper third of the oven for 6 hours. The tomatoes should be dried and crinkly, wrinkly but not burnt or crispy. You want them leathery on the outside and moist on the inside. Set aside.

For the roasted onions: Preheat the oven to 350ºF. Leaving the trimmed root on, cut 2 onions top to bottom in half, and then cut each half in thirds so the onions don't fall apart. Place the onions in a large bowl. Add 1 tablespoon olive oil and mix gently by hand. Season with salt and pepper. Place in a baking pan, and bake until brown and starting to appear charred. Set aside.

"Emilia" Burger with Salsa Verde and Balsamic Mayo
Massimo Bottura celebrates Columbus Day with Parmigiano-laced burgers.
MAKES 4

We've always admired Massimo's Italian blend of whimsy and creativity. After all, his Osteri Francescana in Modena is considered among the best restaurants in the world. So when Massimo offered to create a special burger for Columbus Day to commemorate his roots in Emilia Romagna, how could we say no?

Heat the oil in a large frying pan over medium-high heat. Once hot, add burgers to pan and cook until well seared, 2–3 minutes per side. Transfer burgers to a cutting board and let rest at least 2 minutes before serving.

To serve, spread bottom of each bun with balsamic mayonnaise, then top with a burger. Spread salsa verde over the burger and top with the bun.

For the Balsamic Mayonnaise: In a small bowl, combine 4 tablespoons mayonnaise and 2½ teaspoons aged balsamic vinegar. Season with salt.

For the Salsa Verde: Pour 2 tablespoons water over 1½-inch-thick slice day-old crusty white bread and allow it to absorb completely. In a blender or food processor, add the soaked bread, 5 tablespoons olive oil, 1 packed cup parsley leaves, 1 tablespoon capers, rinsed and dried, 3 anchovy fillets, ¼ clove garlic, ½ teaspoon white wine vinegar. Salt to taste and purée until smooth. Set aside.

4 hamburger buns, toasted *(page 42)*	Salt and freshly ground black pepper
½ packed cup finely grated Parmigiano-Reggiano	1 tablespoon olive oil
1 pound very cold ground beef	Balsamic Mayonnaise
	Salsa Verde

In a large mixing bowl, fold the grated cheese into the ground beef until uniformly distributed. Lightly season with salt and pepper. Divide the mixture into 4 equal portions and form into ¾-inch thick patties.

Pat LaFrieda's Favorite Burger

Pat LaFrieda *reveals the burger of his dreams.*

My favorite burger recipe is a simple one, for that's what a burger is supposed to be. The quality of meat to be ground, or as we say, chopped, is vital. In fact, I'll only eat burgers whose meat I've produced! The lack of transparency in country of origin, specific cuts used, and by-products in many burgers is frightening.

My meat preference begins with the breed. Black Angus has a consistent flavor profile that captures the salts of the protein with the sweetness of the fat. Animals' age is another huge variable: my beef should be 20 to 24 months old. With older beef, the fat is not as sweet; it sticks to the sides of the grinding machinery and produces a pasty result.

There are vast differences in flavor among the 600 individual muscles in the animal. The cuts selected are important and are chosen for their flavor profiles, pricing structure, availability, or a combination of all these. *(See recommendations, pages 34–35.)*

I prefer an 8-ounce burger, 4 inches in diameter and an inch tall. Because I like a medium-rare center and a seared exterior, my meat goes onto the grill at 38°F, the normal temperature of a refrigerator. Letting meat reach room-temperature can be dangerous. To dress my burger? No ketchup please! American cheese, arugula,

not lettuce, a dollop of mayonnaise, and firm, sliced grape tomatoes. A buttery brioche bun is an indulgent favorite. A bit of extra love right before serving matters: I like to toast the bun before I split it so it's brown on the outside and super-soft inside.

TODAY

tomorrow

@tishacherry

Pedigreed Dogs

General Outdoor Adv Co

"I eat so many hot dogs, I appreciate Vienna's even more. It has just the right amount of snap, a perfect blend of smoke and spice that never overpowers the pure beef."

—MARK ROSATI

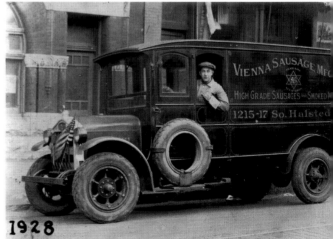

Vienna Beef
CHICAGO, IL

The year 1893 was a proud one for both Vienna Beef and Chicago: it marked the company's founding in the city that hosted the 1893 World's Columbian Exposition, where Vienna's Austrian-Hungarian immigrant founders, Emil Reichel and Sam Ladany, first introduced their family's hot dog recipe. Fast forward to 2001 when Danny (loyal Midwesterner), convinced that Chicago had the best hot dogs, asked Vienna to send samples for that little hot dog cart in the Park. Vienna's pure, all-beef hot dogs (from premium lean beef mixed with brisket trimmings—no hormones or antibiotics—and the founders' original spice blend, smoked over hickory chips, made fresh daily) were a big hit with the initial USHG tasters. They're still served in all domestic Shacks. Vienna developed a Halal version for Middle East Shacks, and today they send enough hot dogs to those Shacks that if laid end to end, they'd stretch 10 miles beyond the distance from Abu Dhabi to Dubai.

PICKLE SPEARS

Kosher dill spears traditionally appeared on early 20th-century Chicago dogs and we love them for the garlicky punch they add to the "dragged through the garden" vegetable toppings.

DICED ONIONS

We love the way the sweet sharpness of diced Spanish onions (another staple of the classic Chicago dog) counterbalances the saltiness of the Vienna Beef dog.

ROMA TOMATOES

Tomato on a hot dog? Another holdover from the Chicago dog, ours are the same Roma tomatoes we serve on ShackBurgers. We love how the warm red half moons give the Shack-cago Dog its signature look.

SPORT PEPPERS

Sport peppers always jazzed up the Chicago dog. Ours has a unique texture. Alone, it's plenty hot, but when it meets the other ingredients, there's just enough heat to make every bite a taste sensation.

CUCUMBER SPEARS

We liven up the garden with a spear of fresh cucumber. We love the cuke's crunch and color pop. Its refreshing cool lets all the other strong ingredients breathe a bit.

Shack-cago Dog

YELLOW MUSTARD

No fancy Dijon here. Good old yellow mustard is just what you put on a hot dog. Come on!

POTATO BUNS

Traditionally, Chicago-style hot dogs are served on a steamed poppyseed bun. But there we had to part ways and champion a signature Shake Shack eating experience, hence Martin's Potato Bun, buttered and toasted.

CELERY SALT

We love how celery salt adds an extra vegetal layer of flavor to the dog. We use it, too, as the last sprinkle on a Chile Dog. It's like a secret ingredient that adds a flavor you can't name.

VIENNA BEEF HOT DOGS

We have used Vienna Beef hot dogs since our first cart in the park in 2001. With Vienna's insistence on the finest ingredients and old-world production, no wonder they're the original Chicago-style dog.

RELISH

We abandoned the Chicago dog's neon relish when we found Rick's Picks' locally sourced relish. We love that it's never too sweet.

Making a Shack-cago Dog ^(at home!)

Splitting the sausage creates even more surface for yummy caramelization.

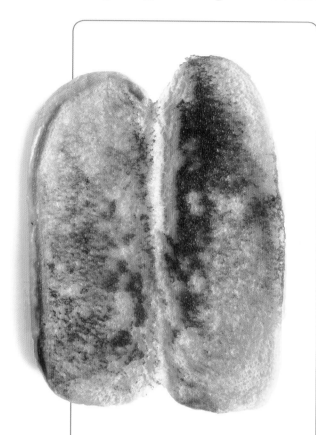

1. Slice the hot dog almost in half lengthwise and open it like a book.

Toasting the Bun

We know, we know. The traditional Chicago-style hot dog bun is covered with poppyseeds and steamed! For years we experimented with all kinds of other buns and cooking methods and we weren't happy until we decided on a griddled potato bun as the proper home for our Shack-cago Dogs.

Brushed inside with melted butter and toasted face down on a hot griddle, this bun adds another layer of culinary delight.

4. Flip the hot dog and cook the other side, about 2 minutes more.

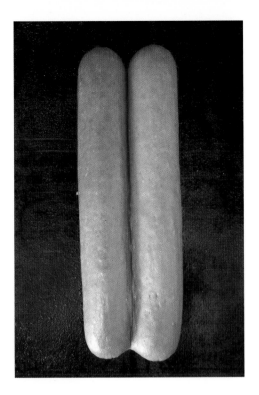

2. Put the hot dog on a hot griddle or cast-iron pan, cut side down.

3. Press down with a large spatula until golden brown, about 2 minutes.

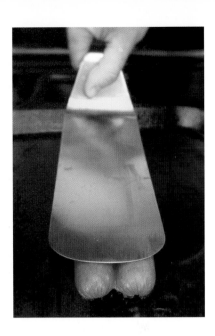

5. Use the spatula to ensure even cooking.

6. Transfer the hot dog to the prepared bun and add your favorite topping.

Shack-cago Dog

MAKES 4

It all started with a hot dog and this is the most iconic of all our menu items. Over the years we've refined the toppings of the classic Chicago-inspired hot dog, and made it our own. But we still hold true to the original maxim: No ketchup! Ever!

4 hot dog potato buns, buttered and toasted (page 92)

4 tablespoons unsalted butter, melted

4 all-beef, high-quality hot dogs

Yellow mustard

8 sport peppers

4 cucumber spears, about ¼ inch thick

4 pickle spears, about ¼ inch thick

4 tablespoons pickle relish

4 tablespoons diced onion

4 ¼-inch slices plum tomato, halved

1 teaspoon celery salt

1. Heat a cast-iron griddle over medium-low heat until warm. Meanwhile, open the hot dog buns and brush the insides with the melted butter. A soft brush is helpful here. Place the buns buttered side down on the griddle and toast until golden brown, 2 to 3 minutes. Transfer buns to a plate.

2. Increase the heat to medium and heat the griddle until hot, 2 to 3 minutes. Meanwhile, cut the hot dogs almost in half lengthwise and open them up like a book. Place them on the griddle cut side down. Cook the hot dogs, pressing down with a large spatula, until they are golden brown, about 2 minutes. Flip the hot dogs, press down again with the spatula, and cook about 2 minutes more.

3. Transfer the hot dogs, cut side up, to the toasted buns. Spoon on the mustard, and add 2 peppers inside each hot dog. Tuck a cucumber spear on one side of the bun and a pickle spear on the other. Spoon relish on one side of the hot dog, and the onions on the other. Top with the tomatoes, sprinkle with celery salt, and enjoy.

@concoquere

Pro Tip

We soak sliced or diced onions in ice cold water for 5 minutes to mellow their sharp flavor, then drain and pile them on dogs or burgers.

LOCAL HERO

Rick's Picks

BROOKLYN, NY

Rick Field grew up in a New England family where pickle-making was as cherished a family value as academics. He worked as a film director in New York for 15 years. Then four things happened: Rick turned 40, lost a job, broke up with a girlfriend, and won a pickle contest. "My therapist told me: 'The world is telling you to start a pickle company.'" Rick decided to try to make a business of his passion, and took a stand at the Union Square Greenmarket, directly in the path of Danny Meyer's daily stroll from the original location of Union Square Cafe and his office. It was 2004, just after Shake Shack launched with a Chicago hot dog with the traditional neon relish. "Yellow #5 is not a good ingredient," says the CEO and Chief Pickler, who's committed to organic, local, and all-natural ingredients. He made Shake Shack a relish they now use worldwide.

Deli Dog

MAKES 4

We created this dog for our Theater District Shack to honor the celebrated Deli history of that neighborhood. Your favorite pastrami will play well here.

- 4 **hot dog potato buns, buttered and toasted** *(page 92)*
- 4 **all-beef, high-quality hot dogs**
- ½ **cup ShackSauce** *(page 49)*
- ½ **cup sauerkraut, warm**
- 4 **slices pastrami, broken in pieces, warm**

Follow the Shack-cago Dog method *(pages 92–93)* and transfer the hot dogs to the buns. Spoon 2 tablespoons sauce on the hot dogs, then the sauerkraut. Top with the pastrami and serve.

The Taxi Dog

MAKES 4

This is one of the original hot dogs sold from that little cart in the Park back in 2001. It's a tried and true classic, but the star of the show is the homemade Tomato-Simmered Onions. If you're a fan of ketchup, try using them on burgers, too.

- 4 **hot dog potato buns, buttered and toasted** *(page 92)*
- 4 **all-beef, high-quality hot dogs**
- 1 **cup sauerkraut, warm**
- 1 **cup Tomato-Simmered Onions, warm**

Follow the Shack-cago Dog method *(pages 92–93)* and transfer the hot dogs to the buns. Spoon sauerkraut along one side of the dogs and the Tomato-Simmered Onions on the other.

Tomato-Simmered Onions

MAKES ABOUT 1 CUP

Heat 1 tablespoon canola oil in a saucepan. Add 1½ onions, peeled, and sliced ¼-inch thick, and cook until soft. Stir in ¼ cup Champagne vinegar, ¼ cup tomato purée, 1 tablespoon tomato paste, ¼ cup water, ¾ teaspoon salt, and a pinch of pepper. Simmer until most of the liquid evaporates and the onions are very soft.

Chili Dog

MAKES 4

A regional Rhode Island classic called the Hot Weiner inspired this dog. Rhode Island chili sauce is a little more watery; ours is thicker and richer.

4 **hot dog potato buns, buttered and toasted** *(page 92)*

4 **all-beef, high-quality hot dogs**

4 **tablespoons mustard**

1 **cup Mark's Rhode Island–inspired Chili Sauce** *(page 146),* **warm**

4 **tablespoons diced onion**

Celery salt

Follow the Shack-cago Dog method *(pages 92–93)* and transfer the hot dogs to the buns. Spoon mustard on the hot dogs, then the chili sauce; scatter the onions on top, sprinkle with celery salt, and serve.

Cheddar Bacon Dog

MAKES 4

Taking time to make this luscious cheese sauce and to seek out a great smoky bacon will transform this hot dog into a show dog.

4 **hot dog potato buns, buttered and toasted** *(page 92)*

4 **all-beef, high-quality hot dogs**

½ **cup Cheese Sauce** *(page 145),* **warm**

4 **slices cooked bacon, crumbled**

Follow the Shack-cago Dog method *(pages 92–93)* and transfer the hot dogs to the buns. Spoon 2 tablespoons sauce on the hot dogs, scatter bacon on top, and serve.

Brewmaster As Director

"The question is, how much style and how much verve can you bring to the form?"

Garrett Oliver has a long relationship with Union Square Hospitality Group heightened in 2006 when Gramercy Tavern launched a vintage beer list that promoted craft beer way before it went mainstream. When Gramercy asked Garrett to come teach their staff about beer, it was only natural that this relationship would spill over into other USHG restaurants, like Blue Smoke, where Brooklyn brewed an Original Ale. Garrett knew Randy from his days running Tabla. So when Randy took over Shake Shack, the obvious step was to brew a special Shack beer. "The thing about Randy," Garrett says, "and what makes his gung ho spirit culturally worthwhile, is that the overall driving spirit, the ethos behind it, is that the thing you're providing is hospitality. The result is for the guest."

Bringing style to the form, Garrett says, "In beer making, just like in the movies, there are basically three plots and the outcome depends on the flair and imagination you bring to it. The most familiar thing is a hamburger; how can you possibly make it something to get excited about? Well, Shake Shack did, and that was our challenge in brewing a beer for them: We're going to make an IPA, but there are 10,000 IPAs in this country. How do we make ShackMeister Ale step out there?

"What does this beer need to be? First, it had to be firm enough to stand up to the ShackBurger's big flavors. A burger is salty and sweet and acidic at the same time, not the easiest combination to pair with. I always ask, 'What am I cutting through, and what am I holding on to?' What I'm holding on to is caramelization, the char of the meat, and the browning of the bun. I'm cutting through fat, and sugar, and for that I need bitterness, enough so that the beer never completely disappears. But you want to leave with a clean palate that doesn't have

any odd flavors hanging around. It needs enough minerality to be bitter enough to be cleansing and it needs to finish dry. It had to be something that a craft beer drinker would like and respect, but also not turn off those who haven't, how shall I say this, made it that far past Heineken yet.

"We nailed it! The most surprising thing about the process was that when Randy and I tasted the burger with the ShackMeister Ale, I think he was kind of shocked. Because we were both, like, 'Bingo!' I think he thought there was going to be a lot of back and forth. I think he was even looking forward to the interplay. And what happened, was, well, I just threw a strike!"

Garrett Oliver *on the banjo, hot dogs, and what to drink with both . . .*

I feel about hot dogs the same way Steve Martin does about the banjo: "It's such a happy instrument, you can't play a sad song on it." A good hot dog never plays a sad song either. As soon as the aroma reaches your nose, it makes you smile. And as soon as the snap of the dog hits your mouth, and the salt and spices light up your tongue, what you want is a beer.

• **Hot Dog with German-Style Pilsner.** With the classic all-beef Vienna dog, it's hard to beat a German-style pilsner. Clean, sharp, straight as an arrow, it plows right down the center of your tongue, melding with mustard, dancing with the extra cheese sauce, putting its soft malts together with the toasty bun. Not a lot of bells and whistles, but if you get a really good pilsner, you don't need them.

• **Bratwurst with ShackMeister Ale.** Aromatic pale ales like the ShackMeister we brew for Shake Shack work so well when you ramp things up with a gutsy Bavarian Bratwurst.

• **Shack-cago Dog with IPAs.** Now it's time to go big. With all those dragged-through-the-garden flavors—relish, onion, pickle, cucumber, tomato, sport pepper, celery salt, and mustard on your dog—it's pretty clear that you've left moderation behind. Time to roll out the IPAs. India Pale Ales are bold, racy, sharply bitter, and explosive with massive floral and citrus flavors. Now you need the IPA flavor riot, as well as the cutting power of hops.

That clean, mineral burst of bitterness, paired with cleansing carbonation, is like a Zamboni for your tongue. Our Shack X IPA, a beer we made for Shake Shack's 10th Anniversary, was definitely the bomb with the Shack-cago Dog, but you can roll with any good full-rigged IPA. Or step it up to a "double IPA," the nickname for beers that are even stronger and bolder than the already hopped-up standard.

Corn Dog

MAKES 4

We bring out corn dogs as our salute to summer. Corn dogs get a bad rap because the ones served up at state fairs are usually too sweet and too greasy. So we reimagined this classic, bringing more balance and spice to the cornbread batter. Now, we must admit, our corn dogs are pretty irresistible.

For the batter:

- 1¾ cups cornmeal
- ¼ cup all-purpose flour
- 3 tablespoons sugar
- 2½ teaspoons kosher salt
- 1 teaspoon baking powder
- ¼ teaspoon baking soda
- Pinch cayenne
- ¼ cup buttermilk
- ½ cup canned creamed corn
- 4 teaspoons diced onion
- 2 teaspoons diced jalapeño
- 4 teaspoons rice wine vinegar
- 1 teaspoon Tabasco Green Jalapeño Sauce

- 4 long wooden skewers
- 4 all-beef, high-quality hot dogs
- 1 cup flour
- Canola oil for deep-frying

1. Combine the cornmeal, flour, sugar, salt, baking powder, baking soda, and cayenne in a large mixing bowl and set aside. Put the buttermilk, corn, onion, jalapeño, vinegar, and Tabasco in a blender and blend until smooth. Add the dry ingredients and blend until smooth. Transfer the batter to a covered container container, and refrigerate at least 6 hours and up to a few days.

2. Insert a long wooden skewer into the center of each hot dog, making sure it goes through the length of the hot dog with enough of the skewer on the bottom to act as a handle. Set aside.

3. Stir the prepared batter well, then fill a tall, narrow glass three-quarters full with some of the batter. This will be used for dunking the hot dogs, so you'll have to replenish the glass with batter.

4. Put the flour on a large plate. Dredge each hot dog in the flour shaking off any excess. Set aside.

5. Pour the oil into a heavy, deep, wide pot to a depth of 6 inches. Heat over medium-high heat until the temperature of the oil reaches 350ºF on a candy thermometer.

6. Working with 1 floured hot dog at a time, dunk the hot dog into the batter, coating it evenly. Pull the hot dog out of the batter, let the excess batter drip off. Then quickly submerge the battered hot dog into the hot oil, holding it by the wooden skewer to keep the hot dog suspended in the oil so it does not stick to the bottom of the pot.

7. Once the batter begins to form a crust, about 30 seconds, release the corn dog into the oil. It should float. Fry the corn dog, turning it halfway through, until the crust is deep golden brown, about 3 minutes. Drain on paper towels. Serve hot.

Corn Dogs are a special treat for Caleb, Keira, and Connor Garutti, at their neighborhood Upper West Side Shack.

Currywurst

MAKES 4

Curry is prized in Europe where curry sauce on sausages is such a thing; it's sometimes served on top of French fries, too. Our version has plenty of sauce, and to add that crispy crunch, we go for fried shallots, marinated in our ShackMeister Ale. 'Cause beer and sausages is a thing, too.

4 **hot dog potato buns, buttered and toasted** *(page 92)*	1 **recipe ShackMeister Fried Shallots** *(page 62)*
4 **bratwursts**	
½ **cup Curry Tomato Sauce**	

Follow the Shack-cago Dog method *(pages 92–93)*, but cook the sausages 3 minutes per side. Transfer the sausages to the buns. Spoon 2 tablespoons of the sauce onto the sausage, top with the fried shallots, and serve.

If it's fall, it's Shacktoberfest, our annual celebration of beer and brat-loving German traditions, with a special bier stein for copious amounts of Brooklyn Brewery's brews, Bavarian-inspired frozen custard, and a variation of a strudel Shake.

Curry Tomato Sauce

MAKES ABOUT 1¼ CUPS

Smoked paprika adds a wonderful depth to this classically inspired ketchup-based curry sauce. Lemon juice adds a welcome brightness.

2 **teaspoons canola oil**	½ **teaspoon smoked paprika**
2 **tablespoons diced onions**	1 **cup ketchup**
⅛ **teaspoon kosher salt**	½ **teaspoon fresh lemon juice**
1½ **teaspoons Madras curry powder**	

Heat the oil in a medium saucepan over medium heat. Add the onions and salt and cook, stirring often, until soft, about 5 minutes. Add the curry and paprika and cook until fragrant, about 1 minute. Stir in ½ cup water, ketchup, and lemon juice. Bring to a simmer and cook until the sauce thickens slightly, about 10 minutes. Sauce will keep, covered and refrigerated, for about 1 week.

Bavarian Bratwurst

MAKES 4

Fall is bratwurst weather at Shake Shack, and our annual Shacktoberfest celebration features variations of the smoky brats, served with an assertive, grainy mustard, and sauerkraut, or our version of German-style slaw.

- 4 **hot dog potato buns, buttered and toasted** *(page 92)*
- 4 **bratwursts**
- 1½ **cups German-Style Slaw**

Follow the Shack-cago Dog method *(pages 92–93)*, but cook the sausages 3 minutes per side. Transfer the sausages to the buns. Spoon lots of slaw onto the sausages and serve.

German-Style Slaw

MAKES ABOUT 1½ CUPS

What if slaw was made with sauerkraut instead of raw cabbage and ShackSauce not mayo? Wunderbar!

- ½ **cup ShackSauce** *(page 49)*
- 1 **tablespoon whole-grain Dijon mustard**
- 2 **teaspoons honey**
- 1 **teaspoon fresh lemon juice**
- 1 **pound sauerkraut, well drained**

Mix the sauce, mustard, honey, and lemon juice together in a medium bowl. Add the sauerkraut and stir until well combined.

Usinger's

MILWAUKEE, WI

Shake Shack has a tradition of choosing venerable family-owned American businesses to supply quality foodstuffs. And since Danny grew up in St. Louis on Usinger's bratwurst and braunschweiger, we've used their products since day one. Currently run by fourth-gerneration Fritz Usinger, the company began when Fritz's great-grandfather Frederick (who learned sausage-making, appropriately enough, in Frankfurt, Germany) moved to Milwaukee in the late 1870s, married the niece of a butcher shop owner, and launched the dynasty that still bears his name. We roll out Usinger's smoky veal and port bratwursts, with their snappy natural casings and tender interiors, every fall at Shacktoberfest celebrations in special editions that include Bavarian Brats, Cheddar Brats, and Currywursts.

Publican Sausage

MAKES 4

The pork sausages Publican Quality Meats make for us are made in the refined style of Southwestern France, with fresh thyme and white wine, and lightly smoked just for Shake Shack. Most neighborhoods have artisanal butchers who turn out similarly fine sausages.

4   **hot dog potato buns, buttered and toasted** *(page 92)*

4   **Publican sausages, or other fine pork sausages**

½   **cup Cheese Sauce** *(page 145),* **warm**

4   **ounces ShackMeister Fried Shallots** *(page 62)*

Follow the Shack-cago Dog method *(pages 92–93),* but cook the sausages 3 minutes per side. Transfer the sausages to the buns. Spoon on 2 tablespoons of the cheese sauce, scatter the fried shallots on top, and serve.

LOCAL HERO

One Off Hospitality
CHICAGO, IL

Paul Kahan had a great deal to do with changing the contemporary dining scene in Chicago, founding a company with his partners called One Off Hospitality that makes each of his restaurants feel special, of its time and place: from the unpretentious and excellent Blackbird, launched in 1998, to Big Star Tacos, from the small plate wonder Avec to the award-winning bar The Violet Hour.

"Their restaurants," says Eater.com's national restaurant critic Bill Addison, "whether they lean fine dining or casual, hit big with diners but never spiral into kitsch or ubiquity." Publican is Kahan's German-inspired beer hall, and right across the street is the group's butcher shop, Publican Quality Meats. There, Paul and his chef de cuisine, Cosmo Goss, make flavorful pork sausages like those at our Chicago Shacks, finessed with fresh herbs and white wine.

WINE WITH HOT DOGS

• **Shack-cago Dog with Rosé.** The phrase "Chicago dog" conjures hilarious memories of Bill Swerski's Super Fans and Chris Farley in a grass skirt. It means pairing a wine with a food that's salty, sweet, pickled, and mustardy (NEVER ketchup). That tall order is readily met by a glass of rosé. Yes, real rosé from Provence, or even better, our Frog's Leap La Grenouille Rougante "Pink." With its high acid and bright strawberry-meets-rhubarb fruit flavors, this unlikely combo of the manliest of foods and the most delicate of wines is such an odd and stellar pairing that it could even make Mike Ditka forsake his beloved Polish Sausage!

• **Corn Dog with Chenin Blanc.** The question of what to pair with a Corn Dog has haunted me for years. A Corn Dog is a symphony of flavors: the sweet cornbread coating, the crispy exterior harmonizing with the salty, meaty snap of the dog. And the wine that pairs well with these attributes? The oft-overlooked Chenin Blanc! In 2015, for the first time, we made Shack White from Chenin Blanc. This wine is floral and fruited, high-toned and bright, matching the Corn Dog note for note.

—*Jonah Beer, Frog's Leap*

A Culture of "Yes"

We're in the "Feel" Business

By Randy Garutti

Shake Shack has always been about "moving mountains." It's a deliberate striving for excellence that began intuitively; it was just the way we did business. But as we've grown, our culture had to be shared, articulated, and intentional. Danny taught us that. But when it comes to moving mountains, I guess I learned that growing up. My mom taught me to never see obstacles in life, to push through to the next challenge, and to believe there's nothing you can't achieve. When my brother and I were 8 or 9 years old, she'd call and tell us, "There's chicken in the fridge, cook it up and have it ready for dinner when I get home!" If there was work to be accomplished, saying "No" was not an option. She just expected us to get stuff done. And have fun doing it.

My dad taught me to always believe in me—no matter what! He gave me intellectual curiosity and inspired me to *want* to learn, to ask why, to never let the status quo be good enough, to take my thinking to the next critical level. And to do it all with passion!

If I were to interview you for a job today, I'd look you in the eye and say: "There's something you have to know to work here. Moving mountains is the baseline requirement of your job. And if that's not for you, then this place isn't for you." Today, Shake Shack's attitude reflects that. We believe anything's possible. We work to make things just a little bit better each day. We are realistically confident that anything can be achieved, and we work hard to find the "Yes!" in every interaction.

Randy and the team
at the opening of the
first Tokyo Shack in
Meiji-Jingu Gaien Park.

We push each other, too. I was lucky to be born with a positive mind-set. I wake up every day believing this day could be the best day of my life. But that attitude has downsides I'm well aware of. I don't wake up worried about the world, so it's important that I surround myself with a few people who do. I love it when our team pushes back and together we find a better answer. I surround myself with leaders who are different, who want to find great solutions and who share the common desire to make Shake Shack just a little better today than yesterday.

The bigger we get, the smaller we need to act. We believe that each time we add a link to our chain, we do it with the same attention to detail, the same passion, and the same creativity as the first. Who ever wrote the rule that a "chain" couldn't be a positive force for good? We believe we're building something special—a "chain" that becomes even stronger as it grows.

We challenge the givens, every day. It's why we grind your burger fresh every night from only the best cuts of hormone-and-antibiotic-free beef using only whole muscles, never trimmings. We spin your milkshake by hand, made from our own frozen custard that's made fresh all day. We use the finest ingredients—many shared in this book—to make our favorite versions of the classics you love. We work with the best local purveyors and tell them with confidence, "You'll grow with us as we grow." We love to challenge conventional wisdom. And prove it wrong!

Hospitality. At the core of our team training is our favorite quote from the great Maya Angelou, who said, "People will forget what you said, people will forget what you did, but people will never forget how you made them feel." Since day one, we've been in the "feel" business, re-creating and undoing everything people were wired to believe about traditional fast food. Somehow, when we put that all together, the Shack creates a natural, effortless connection that people gravitate toward. It's a defining thing, not

@janelikesme

"The bigger we get, the smaller we need to act."

—RANDY GARUTTI

an intellectual construct. It's something people all over the world can put their arms around. It's easy and it's fun. It just feels right when you're together at the Shack with the people who matter to you. You enter with excited anticipation, and you leave feeling just a little bit happier.

We stand for something good. And we're doing it one burger at a time. At the end of the day, my ultimate role and the role of our leaders is to surround ourselves with amazing human beings and create an environment where A+ people make the right decisions. When we do that, magical things happen. As Danny Meyer says, "It's that simple. And it's that hard."

Not Just "Flipping Burgers"

I was asked to speak at a conference held by Conscious Capitalism, an organization devoted to mindful business practices and supported by the likes of Whole Foods and The Container Store. As I was finishing my speech, I knew that my team was working hard outside preparing burgers for an unsuspecting crowd of 200 CEOs, presidents, and industry leaders.

We had spent much time the previous two days talking about taking care of our people. On a panel about the importance of the minimum wage, I'd told them that nothing upsets me more than hearing the term "flipping burgers" to designate the lowest form of work. I'm proud of our hardworking team. We are a career choice for many, a

place to start, or restart. A place to build confidence and ultimately a place that can lift you up even further.

So as I finished my speech, I told the crowd, "My team is outside cooking burgers for you. But guess what? You're not going to get one until you do me a favor." Then I asked, "When was the last time you looked at a person in the eye who flipped your hamburger, thanked them, and gave them the dignity they deserve?" I got choked up. People immediately went behind the tent to shake hands with our crew. It was awesome, a real example of if we really believe what we preach, maybe we can push the world a little bit. Maybe next time you grab a burger in your hometown, you'll do the same.

"I challenge you to put us out of business with your generosity."

—RANDY GARUTTI

SHACK PACT

What We Do:
We Stand For Something Good

Who We Are:

We Are Boundless Hospitality

We follow the 5 Tenets of Enlightened Hospitality.
We smile a lot, listen closely and use every interaction to enrich our culture.
We always find the "yes" and write the next great chapter in real time.
The bigger we get, the smaller we act.

We Are a Team – We Take Care of Each Other

We are 51%ers committed to championship performance.
We honor our schedules and commitments, arrive ready and leave only after packing parachutes.
We drive change to improve, and always offer solutions.
We communicate positively, give and receive constructive feedback and constantly seek to develop ourselves while teaching others.
We balance fun and humor with respect, trust and integrity.
We compensate our teams with competitive pay, rich benefits and meaningful opportunities.
We have leaders who take on larger roles, travel the world and competitively earn Shacknowledgments.

We Are Fine Casual – Inspired Food & Drink

We cultivate our fine-dining roots and elevate classic roadside burger stand fare.
We responsibly source ingredients, and thoughtfully put them together to make delicious food.
We focus on our core menu while always innovating.
We balance speed of service with photo-ready presentation.
We collaborate with award-winning chefs, talented bakers, responsible growers and great like-minded companies.
We push to do what others are unwilling or unable to do.

We Are a Warm Community Gathering Place

We thoughtfully design Shacks to mirror their distinct neighborhoods.
We engage with our community, inside and outside the Shack, in line and online.
We are a destination for little league champions, study sessions, birthdays, business meetings, run clubs, midday breaks, engagements, late-night hangs, first dates, fifth dates and family nights.
We keep our Shacks in tiptop shape, and they are clean and welcoming for new and returning guests.
We nurture and grow our beloved brand, create conversations and foster deep enriching relationships with our fans.

We Are Accountable for Results

We practice the Excellence Reflex and take zero shortcuts.
We plan for the business we want, and are responsible for the business we have.
We keep everyone safe with diligence in maintenance, cleaning, sanitation and hygiene.
We invest in ourselves, our company and our Shacks.
We make money and use profits to create opportunities for all of our stakeholders.
We strengthen our brand with every decision, our long-term goals are believed and our company is held to higher standards than others.

That "Look 'Em in the Eye" Attitude

"There's not a whole lot of direction out there for kids. Their employment may be the only place for them to blossom."

—PEGGY RUBENZER, SVP, PEOPLE RESOURCES

When Randy hired Peggy Rubenzer from deep management experience at Southwest Airlines and then PF Chang's, there was no consistent process in place for promotion and pay increases. Each Shack managed their people differently. "I wanted to make sure that the brand our employees experience is consistent with the brand our guests experience," she explains. "I wanted to help create a culture that breathes more life and more passion and more energy into the things they do every day." Peggy began to design accessible online training modules, where employees can engage at their own pace. "I went through training, learning every job like a new hire would.

"You know those companies that slap five values on a wall and hope that becomes the culture? Not for us. We know that each person you bring into your culture somehow changes it. So we created a course that says, 'This is how you get promoted.' We call it our Steppin' Up model because through their own initiative our team members step up to the next level of pay and responsibility. You click into Station Training, and you can learn every station in the kitchen. Two certifications and you get a training title and a pay increase. And upward through six certification steps. We wanted to show there's a reason why you're getting more money and a better title. We remove the randomness, provide crystal clear direction and opportunity, and say, 'Now it's up to you!'"

Cross-training spreads the culture. Team members qualify to be sent to train teams for weeks at each new Shack worldwide.

"People will forget what you said. People will forget what you did. People will never forget how you made them feel."

—MAYA ANGELOU

LEADERS TRAINING FUTURE LEADERS

A Day in Her Life
"I want everyone to drink the Kool-Aid like I did."
—RUTH ALCEUS, ASSISTANT GENERAL MANAGER, ATLANTA

In 2010, Ruth Alceus was working at a Burger King in Miami Beach, living with her six kids in a sketchy neighborhood, when she saw an online ad that Shake Shack was opening. "I didn't even know what it was, and I certainly was not thinking of advancing," she remembers. Nonetheless, she interviewed with Zach Koff (now Chief Operating Officer, but then GM of his first Shack) and was hired. "Once I saw how they did things, how people communicated with each other, that made me think outside the box. Randy and Danny came to work with us and I thought 'When does a CEO and chairman just show up like that?' I got to know the people who came to cross-train us. I saw that they were regular people like me, but they were traveling the world. And I began to think I could do better things, too. It was pretty cool, and life changing."

Two years later, when Coral Gables opened, Ruth was ready to be a manager, and moved there with her family. And in 2014, Ruth

122

1. On duty. 2. Home training. 3. Youngest kids at 5:30 a.m. 4. Helping Berverlie Dumas on custard. 5. Buckhead. 6. GM Josh Kalson talks new hires. 7. Calming a guest whose order is "in the red" over 7 minutes. 8. Six kids make dinner at home.

moved to Atlanta to help open the first Shack there, in Buckhead. "I always wanted to live here," she says. "It makes a difference for my kids. For everything."

"Anytime somebody comes to me with a problem, whether it's work-related or not, I'm always listening. It's part of my job to train and encourage our employees, to put out positive energy, to work with them one-on-one, to help set training goals and then help them reach those goals. I try to pay attention to all the little details; I watch their facial expressions. We try to keep it fun, but this is work! I was on the line, I get it. I know what 'we are really busy right now' means. It makes me a better boss. Today a guest dropped his shake. Twice! We just made him another. And another." When the next Atlanta Shack opened, Ruth became its Assistant General Manager!

Stand for Something Good

From the sale of its first hot dog in Madison Square Park, community outreach was baked into Shake Shack's culture. That impulse is interpreted in myriad ways as every Shack in the world chooses its own initiatives, donating time through Shack Gives Back volunteer programs and partnering with charities as big as the March of Dimes and No Kid Hungry *(page 206)* and as hyper-local as in Austin's efforts to clean up Lady Bird Lake, the Miami Beach team's visits with kids at the Miami Children's Hospital, Philadelphia's commitment to the city's Mural Arts Program, and Washington D.C.'s support of the Woolly Mammoth Theater Company.

In Tokyo, Meiji-Jingu Gaien Shack partners with Hokogo Npo After School, whose mission is to provide a safe and stimulating environment to children without a place to go. What do they do? Cook of course. And practice their English.

Every bottle of Shack2O natural spring water funds 1% for the Planet, a global movement begun by Patagonia's founder Yvon Chouinard, among others, that supports The Waterkeeper Alliance and the cleanup of water sources around the world.

Shack Track & Field

It began innocently enough. Allan Ng, a North Carolina boy, came to Philadelphia as General Manager, charged with opening the first Shack there. "We had to win the city of Philly. They have a lot of pride," he recalls. "No one knew about us. It was exhilarating but exhausting work."

One day, Allan, a runner, pinned a note to the office door: "'Hey, I'm going for a run, wanna come?' A few people came out, and everyone had perma-smiles, everyone was sweating and happy." What swiftly became Shack Track & Field has grown organically into a free community fitness club with runs and yoga classes and bike rides in cities nationwide. With branches in Moscow. And London. With its own Facebook page. And logo. And T-shirt. And partnership with SoulCycle. Marriages have begun there. It was the start of something good.

Going Public: We Love What We Do and Want to Do It More Often

"Why would you want to ruin your business by going public?" Randy was asked recently, at one of the many investor meetings he attends, where, he says, he gets routinely questioned by Wall Street who "relentlessly pressure us to grow! grow! grow! . . .

"Nowadays, even the responsible growth we practice requires money. And while there are many ways to get it, for us, the best way to grow was to become a public company. What it takes to be a great public company

is the desire to actually execute growth: a company needs a real fervor and excitement around it so it will never *stop* growing. When you think about Shake Shack as the next generation of the burger joint, an IPO was the way to help us rocketship into that place.

"But I have a favorite answer to that question, and that is this: Truly, becoming a public company was the best way to create opportunity for the people that got us here and the people who I firmly believe will

> *"A crucial truth that gets lost in the hubbub around an IPO is that the business can now be owned in part by its greatest fans."*
>
> **—DANNY MEYER & RANDY GARUTTI**, *Letter to Shareholders*

take us in the direction we want to go.

"Shake Shack was born in a public park: As of January 29, 2015, it could actually be owned by the public. For Shake Shack, going public is a way to spread the culture we believe in. For our team, growth means so many more jobs at more income levels; it's a way to keep more farmers and artisanal producers in business; a way to raise even more money for the charities and causes we believe in and support.

"Our brand is so personal; people are always telling us: 'I want a Shake Shack in my town!' Now they can take ownership of it. We've always been incredibly grateful for the people from all walks of life who genuinely love us, and who already feel like Shake Shack is theirs. What we're really excited about is that now it actually can be. Our goal is nothing less than to be one of the best companies in the world, for the world, and for our team. Now let's eat!"

127

Chapter

5

Oh Those Crinkle Cuts

Into the Fryer...

Danny Meyer has a saying (well, he has many of them): "The road to success is paved with mistakes well handled." And though he didn't coin that one about Shake Shack's adventures with fresh cut fries, he might as well have. As Randy recalls it, "We first chose the crinkle cut fry because it was classic, reminiscent of childhood. And because we had no space. Of course we had to do a frozen fry, because we were in some goofy little kiosk." There were grumbles, but it wasn't until February 2012, when *New York Times* restaurant critic Pete Wells famously asked why Shake Shack couldn't make a decent French fry, that Randy and Mark Rosati launched a soul-searching journey. They were convinced that fresh cut fries were the answer.

Mark: To make the switch to fresh cut fries, Jeff Amoscato and I flew around the country looking at potato farms, meeting farmers, testing: Back in New York, culinary manager Gillian Ortiz and I would fry fresh potatoes and get perfect batches— golden brown and crunchy and crisp. The next day, they'd be over-caramelized, burnt, and soggy. We couldn't figure out what was going wrong. Once we found a farm that would be crazy enough to actually check the sugar content of potatoes before they sent them to us, we thought we had it. Then we discovered

"My job was to get fresh fries into all the Shacks. We started with something that wouldn't necessarily work and basically what we did was to get it to not necessarily work everywhere."

—ZACH KOFF, CHIEF OPERATING OFFICER

> # "Mr. Meyer runs one of the world's great restaurant companies. Can't one of his chefs show him how to make a decent French fry?"
>
> — PETE WELLS, RESTAURANT CRITIC
> *The New York Times, 2/22/12*

the rail car wasn't heated. So it'd be going through the Midwest in the winter, the train would stop, all that cold air would get to the potatoes and make the sugar level spike. We'd get to the Shack, cook the fries, and again: dark brown.

Randy: We found the path of the potato could not be controlled. In reality, we discovered that the fresh fry cannot be made right every day, every time. Mark was doing all kinds of different crazy things. Vinegar, marinating—thrice fried . . .

Mark: Thrice fried came out of spending time in London and tasting Heston Blumenthal's fries (he's the 3-star Michelin chef of The Fat Duck). His were the best fries I'd ever had. The more research I did, it turned out his process was not unlike what a big fry manufacturer would do: water blanching to start to cook the potato and set the starches, give it that nice crispiness on the outside, and then freeze it. Heston loved freezing potatoes so the ice crystals would explode, creating a mashed potato–like inside.

> *"We do things that others are unwilling or unable to do."*
>
> **—RANDY GARUTTI**

Randy: Refrigerating, not refrigerating. Name your favorite thing, we tried it. And Mark and Gillian perfected it: twice fried, soaked until the starch ran out, and washed until the water ran clear.

Mark: The real magic was in developing a process the Shacks could actually execute. We had these giant bins made with casters, so we could cut potatoes into them, fill them with water, then roll them into the walk-in. We had to pull them out and drain the water. Such a nightmare.

Randy: We spent over $1 million on this experiment. And that's just equipment. I'm not talking about the emotional pain.

Mark: Oh, no price on that.

Randy: For the famous launch day, we made T-shirts that said, "Heard" and I actually delivered a note to Pete Wells (a year and a half after his review) with a T-shirt, "Pete, Heard." Everyone in the Shack wore them. On day one, I served fries at the Upper East Side Shack, but I might as well have been going twelve rounds with Mike Tyson. I'll never forget the woman who said, "You have ruined my life with these fries. I will never be back."

Mark: The best was the very first guest at the Upper East Side, day one. I was with our team on the front line, ready to cook the first order of fries. Big smiles on our faces. Guy walks in and orders the fries. We're all watching to see his reaction. He goes nuts: "What the hell is this? These aren't your fries! You guys are becoming too big and too corporate. I want my money back!" And we're thinking how un-corporate and crazy this really was.

Randy: Over the course of a year, we converted the whole company to fresh cut fries. And the divided camps began. It

We were sure we were doing the right thing by converting to fresh cut fries.

was "They're so great," or, "What are you thinking? These are terrible." Meanwhile, in the Shacks, our best people on the front lines were relentlessly under fire from angry customers. The potato cutting devices were falling off the wall. Because once you cut 2,000 potatoes (and that's just in one day) . . .

Mark: We were literally ripping them out of the wall.

Randy: So now, we can't cut potatoes; water's spilling everywhere; people were getting injured. Everything bad was happening, and our response was "No, no, no, people. We know better." We were unyielding while our guys were taking the heat. Then we began to doubt ourselves. But no one would admit it, because my leadership style is to keep going forward. I'm a pretty good listener, but nobody's going to tell me we made a bad million-dollar decision here. And Danny? He was with us at the outset, so he wasn't about to admit that he was bummed out, too.

Meanwhile, I'm doing taste tests with my kids and they tell me they like crinkle cuts better. So two things happened, in the same weekend. An Instagram post appears from Jessica Seinfeld, Jerry's wife, who's a talented cookbook author. They'd ordered burgers to their Little League game in Central Park. Her post said, "Thank you, Shake Shack, we love you, but PS, can we talk about these fries at some point?" And some guy responds to her saying, "Yeah, can you just tell Danny Meyer we don't care about fresh fries, we just want 'em to taste good?" And, at that moment, I remember thinking, "What are we doing here?"

That same weekend, I ordered burgers for my kids' last Little League game. **And I chose not to order fries.** I, myself, don't order

At the time, this was our most-liked Instagram ever, when we announced the return of crinkle cuts.

them because I know deep down the kids don't want 'em. At the end of that weekend, I called Danny and said, "I think we screwed this up." And it felt like an existential moment, like someone who's finally come clean about something they've always wanted to come clean about.

Mark: As soon as we heard this, we all said "Thank God."

Randy: So in mid-2014, we decided to go back to crinkle cuts. Then I challenged the team: How can we go back better? How can we stand for something good here? And the beauty of the timing was in that whole last year of this process, in London, we had launched a crinkle cut fry that had none of the preservatives or coloring of the original Shack fry. So we took that learning, applied it here, and relaunched.

Mark: The food requirements in London meant we were already making those fries. But we could not import them. Our fry company has a big plant in the U.K. So we reached out to them and asked, "Could you possibly give us a better frozen fry as an alternative in the U.S.?"

Randy: One of the other lessons here is that it's important to say that we allowed a few loud voices to lead us to believe there really was this groundswell of people who didn't like the crinkle cuts. That's where we were just wrong. Were there voices? Of course there were. They were loud. And I didn't listen to my people who were good soldiers and followed me, even when it all started to go wrong. What we learned is that we had ten years of people who loved crinkle cut fries. So shame on us for over-intellectualizing the whole thing.

Above, harvest at Lamb Weston 100 Circle Farms, in Washington's Columbia River basin. Freshly dug potatoes go from field to truck to the plant to be washed, cut, and made into French fries in a few hours. Right, potato fields in bloom in Idaho's Snake River Valley. Opposite above, our Yukon potatoes. Opposite below, Low Line Canal in Idaho's Magic Valley, another rich potato-growing region.

LOCAL HERO

Lamb Weston

COLUMBIA RIVER BASIN, WA

Our potatoes for fries have had a nice life, grown as they are on farms in Washington State along the Columbia River Basin. Lamb Weston, as described by Dave Smith, manager of long-term innovation, is a company that "has their hands in the dirt, with a world view of sustainability, mindful of water resources. We know our land has to be productive forever: we can't ruin it!" Lamb Weston's 100 Circle Farms form those vast, sweeping crop circles you've looked down on from airplane windows. It's said they're even visible from space! Potatoes are grown along with herds of dairy cattle, who then feed on the harvested potato plants, making a virtuous circle. The potatoes we use are large and yellow or gold fleshed.

Anatomy of

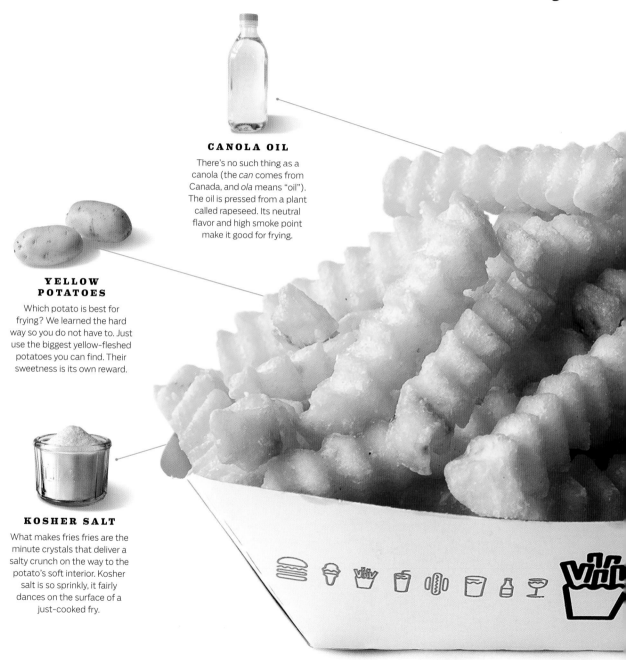

CANOLA OIL

There's no such thing as a canola (the *can* comes from Canada, and *ola* means "oil"). The oil is pressed from a plant called rapeseed. Its neutral flavor and high smoke point make it good for frying.

YELLOW POTATOES

Which potato is best for frying? We learned the hard way so you do not have to. Just use the biggest yellow-fleshed potatoes you can find. Their sweetness is its own reward.

KOSHER SALT

What makes fries fries are the minute crystals that deliver a salty crunch on the way to the potato's soft interior. Kosher salt is so sprinkly, it fairly dances on the surface of a just-cooked fry.

Crinkle Cut Fries

CRINKLE CUTTER

Yes you can cut your potatoes like a pro. We tried lots of cutters, but this U-shaped wonder was the easiest to use and sturdy enough for those big Yukons.

When You Just Can't Get to a Shack

Let's admit it: Our fries are always better at a Shack! But we did experiment with making crispy fries at home so you didn't have to! Thinking like restaurant cooks, our experience making excellent fries with heavy-duty deep-fat fryers naturally led us to investigate the electric home version. And though the machine, below, is nifty, we were delighted (and relieved) when a heavy, deep pot and a good (readable) candy thermometer proved easier to use (and store) and delivered great results.

Making Crinkle Cut Fries (at home!)

It's easier than you think to make crispy French fries in your kitchen.

1. Peel potatoes, and submerge in a bowl of cold water to keep them from turning brown.

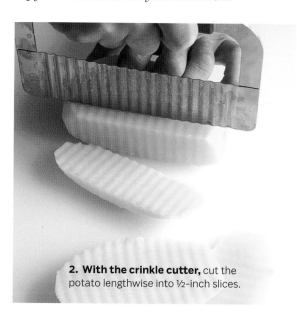

2. With the crinkle cutter, cut the potato lengthwise into ½-inch slices.

6. Pour canola oil into a heavy, deep pot and heat until 350°F. Working in batches, fry until potatoes are pale gold and tender, 10 to 12 minutes. Drain.

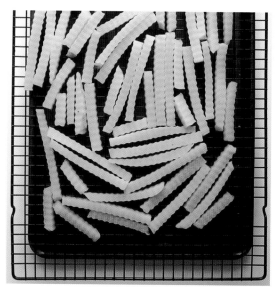

5. Transfer the boiled fries to a wire rack to drain and cool. Pat with paper towels.

3. Cut each potato slice lengthwise into ½-inch-thick fries.

4. Rinse the fries in cold water, then simmer over medium heat until just tender.

7. Spread the fries on a baking pan and freeze to wick remaining moisture. At this point, they can be frozen in a plastic bag for future frying.

8. Fry in batches in canola oil at 350°F until deep golden brown and crisp. Drain and salt.

@epitomeatl

Crinkle Cut Fries

SERVES 4

There are many easy steps to transform Yukon potatoes into their friable state. It's all spelled out on pages 140–141. When you're ready to fry your crinkle cuts, here's a simple way to do it. We like to fry our potatoes in two batches to maintain the temperature of the oil.

Canola oil for deep-frying

1 pound frozen crinkle cut fries

Kosher salt

1. Pour the oil into a heavy, deep pot to a depth of 4 inches. Heat over medium-high heat until the temperature of the oil reaches 350°F on a candy thermometer.

2. Use a wire spider or slotted spoon to carefully lower the frozen fries into the hot oil. Deep-fry until they're deep golden brown and crisp, 2 to 3 minutes. Transfer the fries to paper towels to drain. Salt and serve immediately.

Irish Fries

SERVES 4

We wouldn't swear that folks eat fries this way in Ireland, but we created Irish Fries as a way to celebrate St. Patrick's Day—and called them When Irish Fries Are Smiling. (Sorry.) The Horseradish Cream is a versatile condiment. Try it on a burger!

Pile 1 recipe of hot Crinkle Cut Fries *(left)* on a platter and spoon the Horseradish Cream over the fries. Scatter 6 slices cooked, diced bacon and ½ cup thinly sliced scallion greens on top of the fries. Serve immediately.

Horseradish Cream

MAKES ABOUT ¾ CUP

Put ½ cup crème fraîche, ¼ cup well drained prepared horseradish, and 2 teaspoons fresh lemon juice into a mixing bowl and stir until well combined. Season with salt and pepper.

Cheese Fries

SERVES 4

Cheese sauce on fries has been a classic from the beginning of time. Once again, we're not giving away our secrets, but we developed this version so you can happily make it at home with available ingredients. Use it on burgers, and hot dogs, and vegetables, too.

Heap hot Crinkle Cut Fries *(page 142)* on four plates. Spoon about ¼ cup of warm cheese sauce over the fries and serve immediately.

Cheese Sauce ← *(close enough)*

MAKES ABOUT 6 CUPS

1 tablespoon canola oil	1 tablespoon white wine vinegar
½ onion, peeled and sliced ½ inch thick	2 teaspoons white wine
6 thin slices jalapeño	2 cups heavy cream
2 teaspoons whole black peppercorns	2 cups grated American cheese
½ teaspoon kosher salt	2 cups grated cheddar

1. Heat the oil in a large saucepan over medium heat. Add the onions, jalapeños, peppercorns, and salt, and cook, stirring often, until the onions are translucent, about 5 minutes. Add the vinegar and wine, and cook until the liquid has almost completely evaporated, about 5 minutes. Stir in the cream. Remove the pan from the heat and let the cream steep for 30 minutes to build flavor.

2. Return the saucepan to the stove and heat over medium heat until very warm (don't let it come to a boil).

3. Meanwhile, put the American and cheddar cheeses into a large heatproof bowl. Pour the hot cream through a strainer (to remove the solids) over the cheeses, stirring until the cheese melts and the sauce is smooth, about 3 minutes. Sauce will keep, covered and refrigerated, for up to 1 week. You can easily reheat the sauce in a microwave or over a pot of gently simmering hot water.

BEER WITH FRIES

• **Fries with Belgian Ale.** When I was a kid, milk was said to be the perfect food, but for me, it was always French fries! Since fries are more Belgian than French, it's no coincidence that Belgian pale ales are perfect with fries. Ale's caramel maltiness enhances the fries' golden crust; its brisk carbonation emphasizes the potatoes' fluffiness.

—*Garrett Oliver, Brooklyn Brewery*

• **Crinkle Cuts & Petit Sirah.** "Can I share your fries?" is a phrase etched into the fear-center of any married man's brain. It means that your wife is about to eat 51% of the fries that were barely enough to satisfy you! I've discovered that if I smother mine in cheese I can knock that percentage down to 33. I've also discovered that fries in cheese sauce pair beautifully with Petit Sirah. The wine's rich texture and brooding fruitiness match the salty crispiness of the fries and all that cheesy goodness. Oh, and, expect 33% of your wine to be "shared" too … so order a second glass from the C-Line.

—*Jonah Beer, Frog's Leap*

Chili Fries
SERVES 4

This is a really unexpected regional recipe. Putting curry spices in a chili recipe is a culinary quirk of the Providence region that Mark grew to love. Heaped on top of fries (or dogs, or burgers, for that matter) this sauce quickly becomes the star.

Heap hot Crinkle Cut Fries *(page 142)* on four plates. Top with warm Chili Sauce and serve immediately.

Mark's Rhode Island–Inspired Chili Sauce
MAKES 3 CUPS

¼ cup canola oil	¼ teaspoon ground allspice
1 onion, peeled and finely diced	¼ teaspoon ground cinnamon
2 tablespoons ancho chili powder	⅛ teaspoon ground star anise
2 tablespoons smoked paprika	1 pound freshly ground beef
1½ teaspoons mustard powder	1 cup beef stock
¼ teaspoon curry powder	1 teaspoon vinegar
	Salt

Heat a medium skillet over medium heat. Add oil and onions and sauté, stirring often, until translucent, about 5 minutes. Stir in ancho chili powder, paprika, mustard powder, curry, allspice, cinnamon, and star anise, and cook until fragrant, about 2 minutes. Add ground beef and cook, breaking it up with a spoon, until it's just browned, about 5 minutes. Add stock and simmer over medium-low heat for 30 minutes. Add vinegar and season with salt.

Bone Marrow Gravy Fries

SERVES 4

Hawksmoor is a wonderful modern steakhouse whose chef Richard Turner, above, and owner Will Beckett were so welcoming to us when we first opened in London. We were inspired by their bone marrow gravy to create our own version. This recipe makes enough sauce to spoon on a nice dry-aged steak like they do at Hawksmoor.

Divide 1 recipe hot Crinkle Cut Fries *(page 142)* among four plates. Spoon about ¼ cup warm Bone Marrow Gravy over the fries and serve immediately.

Bone Marrow Gravy

MAKES ABOUT 4½ CUPS

5 tablespoons unsalted butter, diced	4 tablespoons diced bone marrow, removed from bones
5 tablespoons flour	
2¼ cups beef stock	2½ teaspoons sherry vinegar
Salt and freshly ground black pepper	

3. Remove the pan from the heat and whisk in the vinegar. Strain the gravy through a sieve into a clean saucepan. Keep warm over lowest heat.

1. Melt the butter in a medium saucepan over medium-low heat until just melted. Whisk in the flour and cook, whisking constantly, until the flour mixture begins to turn golden brown and has a nutty aroma, about 3 minutes. You may need to use rubber spatula to scrape the flour mixture out of the corners of the pan.

2. Whisk in the stock until smooth. Add a pinch of salt and pepper. Increase the heat to medium-high and bring to a boil. Reduce the heat to medium and whisk in the marrow, which will melt into the sauce. Simmer the gravy, stirring often, about 3 minutes.

@benononsense

Fresh Cut Fries

Fresh Cut Fries

SERVES 4

We may have gone through our particular hell experimenting with fresh cut fries at the Shacks, but that doesn't mean you can't make great ones at home. We're happy to share our hard-won expertise. Here's how. Fry them twice in small batches. Wait at least 15 minutes and up to 4 hours before frying them again. They're ready for the second fry when the outside of the potatoes looks glazed and shiny.

4 large Yukon potatoes

Canola oil for deep-frying

Kosher salt

1. Use a large, sharp knife to carefully cut each potato lengthwise into ¼-inch-thick slices. Then cut the potato slices lengthwise into ¼-inch-thick sticks. Submerge them in a large bowl of cold water to keep them from turning brown.

2. Rinse the starch from the potatoes under cold running water, drain them, and dry well with paper towels.

3. Pour the oil into a heavy, deep pot to a depth of 4 inches. Heat over medium heat until the temperature of the oil reaches 320ºF on a candy thermometer.

4. Use a wire spider or slotted spoon to carefully lower the fries into the hot oil. Deep-fry the potatoes until they develop a pale golden skin and are tender when pressed between your thumb and forefinger, about 2 minutes. Transfer the fries to a wire rack to drain and cool for at least 15 minutes (and up to 4 hours). Remove the pot of oil from the heat.

5. Reheat the pot of oil over medium-high heat until the temperature reaches 375ºF on a candy thermometer. Working in batches, use a spider or slotted spoon to carefully lower the fries into the hot oil. Deep-fry until they are golden brown and crisp, about 1½ minutes. Transfer the fries to paper towels to drain. Salt and serve immediately.

Fried Pickles

SERVES 4

Fried pickles are a Southern specialty that we developed at the same time as we figured out our fried chicken. They're so fun to eat. Serve them with a variety of toppings, such as ShackSauce *(page 49)*. Or even ketchup!

2	cups round kosher dill pickle slices, drained	½	teaspoon freshly ground black pepper
1½	cups buttermilk		Canola oil for deep-frying
2	cups flour		Kosher salt

1. Soak the pickles in the buttermilk for 5 minutes a large bowl. Whisk together the flour and pepper in a deep wide dish. Set the pickles and seasoned flour aside.

2. Meanwhile, pour the oil into a heavy, deep pot to a depth of 3 inches. Heat over medium heat until the temperature of the oil reaches 350°F on a candy thermometer.

3. Working in batches, dredge the pickles in the flour, shaking off any excess flour. Use a wire spider or a slotted spoon to carefully lower the pickles into the hot oil. Deep-fry the pickles, turning them halfway through, until they are golden brown and crisp, about 3 minutes. Drain on paper towels. Salt and serve immediately.

Hatching a New Classic

Coming Home to Roost

Thursday, January 14, 2016, may have been the first time in the history of Wall Street that a chicken sandwich opened trading on the floor of the New York Stock Exchange. With that opening bell, the new Chick'n Shack was launched. And for us it was a big deal, the first non-beef protein, and the first major menu addition in a decade. New York was having a major chicken moment. That fall, Chick-fil-A had entered the New York market with their biggest store ever. The previous June, David Chang had premiered Fuku, the beginning of a growing empire, serving spicy, batter-fried chicken thighs on a potato bun (daikon slaw optional). One month later, on July 7, only at the three Brooklyn Shake Shacks, we had test-launched Chick'n Shack—an all-natural chicken breast, slow-cooked in buttermilk marinade, hand-dipped in batter, dredged in seasoned flour, fried, then topped with Buttermilk Herb Mayo. The demand was so great that less than 48 hours later, Randy had to announce on Instagram that they'd run out of chicken; the sandwich would be discontinued for two weeks. In three days, those three Shacks had sold more than 5,000 chicken sandwiches.

"We gave ourselves the patience and time with chicken that we did not allow ourselves with fries. Had it not been for that fiasco with fries, we never would have had such a success with chicken."

—ZACH KOFF, CHIEF OPERATING OFFICER

Mark: We knew we needed more chickens! We knew we had something really exciting here, we wanted to bring it back as fast as possible, but then we didn't know if that demand would hold. So we actually took the time to think it through, and agreed: "It's not acceptable to ever run out again." So we said, "Hey guys, we're sorry we ran out, but we promise you, when it comes back, this will not happen again."

Randy: Remember, when we were developing chicken, we were really scarred by fresh fries. This time, there was no way we were going to allow ourselves to launch something that didn't work. We knew that the only way a chicken sandwich could happen was through a scalable solution that was also really tasty—creating a juicy chicken sandwich cooked to order.

SHAKE SHACK

Using a scale of 1-5, with 5 being outstanding, please rate chicken sandwiches based on the following criteria:

Sandwiches		Notes	Taste	Visual Appeal	Crave-ability
1)	Griddled Chicken Breast served on a buttered and toasted potato roll	YUCK DRY		NONE	NO
2)	Griddled Chicken Breast topped with lettuce, tomato and Shack Sauce, and served on a buttered and toasted potato roll	BETTER, BUT STILL DRY			NO
3)	Griddled Chicken Breast, topped with charred onion-cheddar cheese sauce, applewood smoked bacon and served on a buttered and toasted potato roll				
4)	Buttermilk Marinated and Fried Chicken Breast topped with spicy pickles and served on a buttered and toasted potato roll	Good w/ Shack Sauce			
5)	Buttermilk Marinated and Fried Chicken Breast topped with Shack mustard slaw				

Above, the first grilled chicken tasting drew an unenthusiastic rating from Danny. Opposite, Chick'n & Rocky in Philly.

Mark: Two years before that we'd thought about turkey burgers; we had Pat LaFrieda grind us chicken burgers. But we could never get excited about them. Yet we knew beef prices were fluctuating, and we knew we needed a protein alternative. Then we tried grilled chicken, the somewhat healthy option.

Randy: Then Jeff Amoscato found a producer from Chicago who could prepare chicken sous vide [sealed in an airtight bag and cooked in a low temperature water bath that preserves flavor and texture]. And then we had a big tasting with Danny where we were all excited about grilled chicken. And he wrote on his testing sheet: "Yuck. Dry."

Mark: Then we tried fried chicken. That took us another year, because of the great debate over how to do it. We agreed that the best fried chicken had a nice, thick crust, and just taking the sous vide breast out of the bag, tossing it in flour, and frying it was not a great experience. We realized it's the crispy bits that make fried chicken excellent.

Randy: This never would have been possible had we not gone through the fresh fry exercise. Only because we added all those fryers could we make fried chicken. So, talk about a silver lining.

Mark: We worked on so many iterations: Brine? Buttermilk? We knew double-dipping in flour would destroy the fry station with flour everywhere. Finally, we said, what if we just add more buttermilk to the flour and make a thick, crunchy batter?

Randy: Just born out of necessity, we created a better process. And it taught us operation. We went through three different tests at three different Shacks with three different types of equipment. So with chicken, we did everything we didn't do with fries.

Mark: Danny liked fried chicken with ShackSauce, so we started to work on a spicy version. When we showed it to the operators, and they said, "Well, ShackSauce and spicy Shack-Sauce look so similar. What if someone wants spicy ShackSauce on their ShackBurger? How will you tell which is which?"

Randy: This is a really important point, because everybody really loved the spicy ShackSauce. It was ready to go. But this is where operations again forced us to find a better tasting item.

Mark: Which was kind of amazing, 'cause efficiency actually drove creativity.

Randy: Yes. And that was the import- ant moment when Zach called and said, "This is just going to be hard to do." And I said, "Come on, man! Can't you just figure it out?" You know, fresh fries? Just figure it out! That reality check sent us back to the drawing table where we created the buttermilk herb mayo that just made the whole sandwich.

The Taste of Things to Come

Inside the quarterly tasting session, where new menu ideas go to live or die.

Pink shirts are optional at the tasting at Brooklyn's Fulton Street Shack. Tasters, from left, Randy Garutti, Edwin Bragg, Jeff Amoscato, Zach Koff, and Mark Rosati. Left, Senior Culinary R & D Manager Allison Oesterle with Mark.

"Does kale ever belong on a Shack sandwich?"

As the tasting team gathers quarterly to evaluate and debate, the air is thick with questions: "Can we cut sugar in half in drinks like lemonade and 50/50?" "Is the cheese gooey and creamy enough on the new Bacon Cheddar Shack?" "How 'bout shortbread for our new crunchy, non-chocolate Concrete?" "What if we did those big New York pretzels for Shacktoberfest?" Chicken tenders are universally applauded. Not at Shacks yet, but see page 170! And will this group ever find a griddled chicken sandwich to love?

"Why does Shacktoberfest start in September?"

161

Ruprecht Company

CHICAGO, IL

Finding a dependable source for antibiotic-free chicken was the issue that stood between Shake Shack and an alternative protein source. In a chance encounter that proved fortuitous for both, Jeff Amoscato met Ruprecht president Walter Sommers at a trade show.

Ruprecht, said to be the oldest operating food company in Chicago, could indeed provide the quality and quantity of chicken Jeff was eager to find.

Sommers's family had acquired the company in the 1960s, and Walter's leadership had since turned Ruprecht's expertise toward cooking and developing products. Yes they could source antibiotic-free chickens and process the breasts before delivery. This was a perfect solution for Shake Shack, loath to bring another uncooked protein into its kitchens.

Sommers recalls years of experimenting before the eventual rollout: "The first massive testing of the chicken sandwich pitted about thirty different versions against each other."

BUTTERMILK

This miracle ingredient works twice—once as the tenderizing agent in the marinade for the raw chicken breasts and again as the base of the tangy Buttermilk Herb Mayo for the finished sandwich.

SEASONED FLOUR

One of the tricks to achieving the crispiest crust is to add a bunch of baking powder to the flour along with cayenne, smoked paprika, salt and pepper, and a flavor hit of celery salt.

CHICKEN BREAST

We serve only antibiotic-free chicken for all the obvious health reasons and suggest you do, too. Each Chick'n Shack is made with one skinless, boneless chicken breast, about 6 oz. each, halved crosswise.

Chick'n Shack

POTATO BUNS

There's not a softer companion to the crunchy Chick'n Shack than the very same beloved non-GMO Martin's Potato Roll we use with our ShackBurgers.

SHREDDED LETTUCE

We're looking for fresh crunch here against the crispy fried chicken. So we use the bottom half of a head of green leaf lettuce, shredded fine, and layer it on the sandwich.

PICKLES

After lots of tasting, we chose the vinegary crunch of kosher dill pickle slices to balance the richness of the sandwich.

BUTTERMILK HERB MAYO

Not only is the raw chicken marinated in buttermilk, but this Southern-inspired buttermilk mayo is the sauce that makes the difference on the sandwich.

Making Chick'n Shack

(at home!)

At the Shack, we marinate and slow-cook our chicken sous-vide;
you'll come close with this buttermilk double dip.

1. Refrigerate halved
chicken breasts in
Buttermilk Marinade at
least 1 hour and up to
overnight.

2. Dredge chicken breasts
in seasoned flour and set
them aside.

4. Fry the chicken in batches in canola oil at 350ºF until brown and crisp, about 5 minutes.

5. Transfer fried chicken to paper towels to drain.

3. DO IT AGAIN! (This is the trick.) Quickly submerge floured chicken breasts in marinade, and then in seasoned flour.

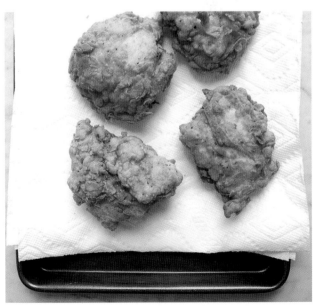

Chick'n Shack

MAKES 4

This recipe may look simple, but getting there took two years! There were so many variables: how to season the flour, the marinade, the sauce? Spicy or sweet? Our core question was: What makes a great chicken sandwich? The chicken! Where to find enough good, all-natural meat? And how to portion it? The ideal for 4 is: 2 thinly sliced skinless, boneless chicken breasts, halved crosswise, about 6 oz. each. At the Shacks we steep the chicken in a tenderizing sous vide bath; at home, it's a buttermilk marinade.

Buttermilk Marinade:
- 2 cups buttermilk
- 1 small shallot, peeled and sliced
- ½ small jalapeño, halved
- ½ small clove garlic, peeled and smashed
- 2 teaspoons salt
- ¼ teaspoon freshly ground black pepper

Seasoned Flour:
- 3½ cups flour
- 4 teaspoons baking powder
- 3 teaspoons kosher salt
- 2½ teaspoons smoked paprika
- 1½ teaspoons freshly ground black pepper
- 1 teaspoon cayenne
- 1 teaspoon celery salt

- 2 thinly sliced, skinless boneless chicken breasts, about 6 oz. each, halved crosswise
- Canola oil for deep-frying
- 4 tablespoons Buttermilk Herb Mayo *(page 170)*
- 4 hamburger potato buns, buttered and toasted *(page 42)*
- 12 round kosher dill pickle slices
- 2 pieces green leaf lettuce, shredded in long strips

For the Buttermilk Marinade: mix together all ingredients in a medium mixing bowl. Set aside.

For the Seasoned Flour: whisk together all ingredients in a deep wide dish. Set aside.

2. Add the chicken breasts to the bowl of buttermilk marinade. Cover and marinate in the refrigerator for at least 1 hour and up to 8 hours.

3. Life one piece of chicken at a time from the marinade, and dredge really well in the seasoned flour, shaking off any excess flour.

4. Return the chicken to the marinade, fully submerge one more time, then dredge again in the seasoned flour. Shake off excess flour and set aside. Discard the marinade.

5. Pour the oil into a heavy, deep pot to a depth of 4 inches. Heat over medium heat until the temperature of the oil reaches 350°F on a candy thermometer.

6. Use a wire spider or slotted spoon to carefully lower the chicken into the hot oil. Fry 2 pieces of chicken at a time until the crust is deep golden brown and crisp, about 5 minutes. Transfer the chicken to paper towels to drain.

7. Spread the Buttermilk Herb Mayo on the bottom of the bun. Add 3 pickle slices and a quarter of the shredded lettuce. Transfer the chicken to the prepared buns and serve.

WINE WITH CHICKEN

• **Chick'n Shack & Chardonnay.** Fried chicken + crisp lettuce + mayo + potato bun = heaven. Add Chardonnay and you've got, well, heaven and a glass of Chardonnay! I love how the tart-meets-tang of the Buttermilk Herb Mayo sauce on the chicken is enhanced by the tart-meets-pomme-fruit of a Chardonnay. Steer clear of an overly buttery Chardonnay, because the wine's characteristic brightness works so well with the savory crisply fried chicken and the sweetness of the bun.

—*Jonah Beer, Frog's Leap*

Chicken Bites

MAKES 4

These crispy bite-size pieces are the
obvious extension of the Chick'n Shack.
We like to make them for a big party (and
for the kids!) served with Buttermilk
Herb Mayo. They're great with our Salt &
Pepper Honey Sauce *(page 173),* too.

2 **thinly sliced
boneless skinless
chicken breasts,
about 6 ounces
each**

Buttermilk Marinade
(page 168)

Seasoned Flour
(page 168)

**Canola oil for
deep-frying**

1 **cup Buttermilk Herb
Mayo, optional**

1. Cut the chicken into thirds lengthwise, then
crosswise into pieces about 2 inches wide.

2. Follow the directions in the Chick'n Shack
recipe *(page 168)* for marinating, dredging, and
deep-frying the chicken pieces.

3. Drain the deep-fried chicken pieces on paper
towels. Serve with the mayonnaise.

Buttermilk Herb Mayo

MAKES 2 CUPS

2 **cups Hellman's
mayonnaise**

2 **tablespoons
buttermilk**

2 **teaspoons white
wine vinegar**

1 **tablespoon finely
chopped parsley**

2 **teaspoons finely
chopped chives**

¼ **teaspoon finely
chopped fresh
thyme**

½ **teaspoon kosher
salt**

¼ **teaspoon freshly
ground black pepper**

Put all the ingredients into a medium mixing bowl
and stir until well combined.

Salt & Pepper Honey Chick'n
MAKES 4

Once we figured out the Chick'n Shack recipe, it opened up a whole range of possibilities. A sweet/savory topping for fried chicken was always in the back of our minds. This honey sauce, so well balanced with salt and pepper, is a great alternative.

6 tablespoons your favorite honey

½ teaspoon salt

¼ teaspoon freshly ground black pepper

4 pieces Chick'n Shack *(page 168)*

4 hamburger potato buns, buttered and toasted *(page 42)*

1. Combine the honey and the salt and pepper in a small bowl and set aside.

2. Place each piece of chicken on a toasted bun and spoon at least 1 tablespoon of sauce on top.

BEER WITH CHICKEN

• **Chick'n Shack & ShackMeister Ale.** Even though ShackMeister Ale preceded the Chick'n Shack by several years, it makes a great pairing. Pilsners and lighter IPAs are nice here too, but what's really fun is how this sandwich brings new beers into the mix. For example, the Chick'n Shack is great with Berliner Weisse and new-fangled "kettle sours," both of them tart with a bright lemony acidity. Now you'll want a second sandwich!

—*Garrett Oliver, Brooklyn Brewery*

Peking Chick'n Shack

MAKES 4

This sandwich is inspired by a collaboration with our friend Erik Bruner-Yang, chef of Maketto and Toki Underground in Washington, D.C. Our idea was to come as close to Peking duck as we could using our Chick'n Shack. We only served it in D.C. for 10 days, but you can make it anytime.

¾ **cup hoisin sauce**

4 **hamburger potato buns, buttered and toasted** *(page 42)*

4 **pieces Chick'n Shack** *(page 168)*

4 **tablespoons sliced scallion greens**

8 **thin slices cucumber rounds**

8 **kosher dill pickle chips**

1. Spoon 1 tablespoon of the hoisin sauce in the center of the bottom bun, and another tablespoon of the sauce on the top bun.

2. Place fried chicken on the bottom bun. Spoon 1 tablespoon hoisin sauce on the chicken, then layer the scallions, cucumbers, and pickles on top.

"We all know how good it feels when that buzzer starts buzzing. We all know how good it feels to be in a pizza parlor and the server comes to your table with your piping-hot pizza. That feeling of anticipation is, as much as anything, at the core of this business."

—**DANNY MEYER**

Fifty-Fifty

MAKES 1 QUART

This drink, sometimes called the Arnold Palmer, is the most thirst-quenching combination. The iced tea tempers the sweetness of the lemonade.

Stir together 2 cups lemonade and 2 cups cold freshly brewed tea in a large pitcher. Keep chilled in the refrigerator. Serve over ice.

Lemonade

MAKES 1 QUART

We've been turning out fresh lemonade since that first hot dog cart in the park. The only thing that's changed is that now we offer a rotating roster of seasonal flavors, such as Strawberry Mint in spring and Peach Lemonade in summer.

Put 1 cup freshly squeezed lemon juice (from about 8 lemons) and 1 cup plus 2 tablespoons sugar into a large pitcher. Stir until the sugar dissolves. Add 3 cups cold water and stir well. Keep lemonade chilled and serve over ice.

Strawberry Mint Lemonade: Add 1/3 cup strawberry puree and 8 large fresh mint leaves to lemonade.

Peach Lemonade: Add 1/2 cup white peach purée to lemonade.

Chapter

7

The Art
of the
Opening

"Wherever we open, we reach out into that new community and strive to bring back exciting local flavors and products— ingredients that celebrate a sense of place."

—MARK ROSATI

California, Here We Come...

As Shake Shack expands into new markets, it is crucial to balance what's well-known and loved about the brand with hyper-local community outreach. Hiring and training are the keys to expanding the culture; seeking out indigenous ingredients keeps each Shack rooted in its specific place. On March 15, 2016, Shake Shack opened in West Hollywood—its first California Shack. It was number 88 worldwide, but in many ways it was a brand new experience.

"The opportunity to launch in California—the roadside burger stand capital of the world—was huge," Randy recalls. "We are hardly a new idea. We didn't invent the burger. And the way we went about this is as true and sincere as the very first Shack we opened. We wanted everybody in that community to feel connected: chefs, bakers, influencers, and, most important, our neighborhood. Mark reached out to chefs he'd long admired in the food community to contribute to Concretes. We planned strategically timed pre-opening events beginning months before, like an outside movie night and a pop-up Shack. If ever there was a 'the bigger we get, the smaller we need to act' moment, it's how we approached Los Angeles.

Interactive Art Walls

We surrounded construction on our first Brooklyn Shack with a Before I Die wall, part of a worldwide movement by artist Candy Chang. In Chicago, it was an interactive sliding puzzle with local landmarks by Noah MacMillan.

"We went into In-N-Out territory with humility. (We all wish we could be In-N-Out when we grow up!) Danny and I sent the message: 'We just hope you put us on your rotation!' 'We just want to be one of your favorites.' We didn't put up signs blaring 'Hey, we're coming to your neighborhood!' Our first step was an art project, the Happy Wall, on the building site on Santa Monica Boulevard. We commissioned a Danish artist, Thomas Dambo, who used 1,600 hinged wooden panels *(page 178)* that exposed color so people could form messages. We wanted to let folks know that we are fun and colorful and eager to interact with the neighborhood. People expressed beautiful thoughts to celebrate Martin Luther King Day and on the day David Bowie died.

"West Hollywood is quite possibly the finest expression of Shake Shack as a community gathering place that we've ever done outside of Madison Square Park. That is a bold statement for me to make. And the results so far bear me out."

"Our mission is to connect with people through their hearts as well as through their stomachs. For LA, our fine dining heritage helped us find the right people to work with. Community spirit happened in a truly organic way."

—EDWIN BRAGG, VP, MARKETING & COMMUNICATIONS

7 WEEKS AHEAD

Son of a Gun Pop-up

Cutting-edge LA chefs Vinny Dotolo and Jon Shook (Animal, Jon & Vinny's), above with Mark, generously turned their Son of a Gun into a Shack pop-up; they did a tuna melt, we did burgers and fries with their malt vinegar aioli. People lined up 100 deep for hours.

7 WEEKS AHEAD
Movie Under the Stars

Even though our parking lot was still a construction site, we turned it into an outdoor movie event among the Dumpsters and backhoes, and screened the original *Star Wars* film. We served ShackBurgers and buttery popcorn caramel custard to about 300 people invited from the neighboring West Hollywood community.

7 WEEKS AHEAD
Backlot Beats & EEEATS Party

We painted walls in Hedley & Bennett's hip apron factory's backyard Instagram-perfect colors (top, and above with our marketing director Laura Enoch and H&B founder Ellen Bennett) and introduced ourselves to 1,200 folks.

3 DAYS BEFORE
Friends & Family

On the Saturday before opening, the new Shack team got to show off where they work. SheRylle Gray (top right), surrounded by her family, has already been promoted to trainer and helped open Hollywood.

THE DAY BEFORE
Opening Night Party

With lights strung across the parking lot meant to recall those at Madison Square Park, big balloons, and the kitchen cranking out trays of three kinds of burgers, WeHo's opening night was sort of toned-down Hollywood style. Lots of food folks, good folks, old friends, and new friends.

SHOWTIME!
Opening Day

"Hospitality is a team sport!" Danny Meyer told the Shack team assembled for a pep talk an hour before they cut the opening ribbon at 11 a.m. "Promote each other," Randy told the group. "Be relentless about each other's success!" "Giving a hug," Danny says, "is the most selfish thing you can do because you get one back." First on the long line that had been gathering on the sidewalk for hours was a guy who flew from New York at 4 a.m. for the opening.

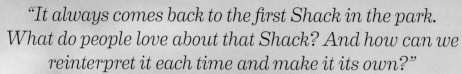

"It always comes back to the first Shack in the park. What do people love about that Shack? And how can we reinterpret it each time and make it its own?"

—MAIJA KREISHMAN, PARTNER

Michael Hsu, Office of Architecture

Michael Hsu, principal of his award-winning Austin-based firm, and his partner, Maija Kreishman, have designed many Shake Shacks. But keeping the original footprint of a building in West Hollywood that housed a chicken rotisserie place called Koo Koo Roo? That was a different challenge. "In WeHo," Maija explains, "we brought that patio out to the street, engaging it with the sidewalk's bustle.

We began with imagery of the way sunlight and shadow filter onto the white walls of California courtyards."

Shake Shack's committment to sourcing the best ingredients comes from their fine-dining mind-set. Michael and Maija's design aesthetic comes from their educated point of view. Neither side dumbs down. "Fast casual has a tendency to make caricatures of design to make it more accessible or more familiar," Michael says. "People think they have to drop quality to reach a big audience. Shake Shack never does that and we never do either."

Rendering by Michael Hsu, Office of Architecture

Sqirl

LOS ANGELES, CA

When Jessica Koslow opened Sqirl in 2011, in the architecturally significant but far-flung Los Angeles neighborhood of Silver Lake, it was as if no one had invented breakfast. Her crispy rice bowls, daily frittatas and quiches, and great slabs of toast with ricotta and jam (served until 4 p.m.!) drew lines for days and turned her little hole in the wall into a community magnet. "I knew I wanted to say Yes! to everything, but I knew I couldn't," is how she describes how she kept it small and unique. "I just had to stay in tune with myself and do what feels right."

What felt right to Jessica began with making small-batch jams of such intense fruit flavor that Mark chose Sqirl Seascape Strawberry & Rose Geranium Jam (sold at the shop), to stir into the Rainbow Connection Vanilla Concrete, named for the West Hollywood neighborhood where it's now served. "Jessica has to be one of the most talented people to cook breakfast ever!" he enthuses, recalling that he was introduced to her two years before they opened in LA.

Larder Baking Co.

LOS ANGELES, CA

There was joy in the land when Suzanne Goin (at right) was named Outstanding Chef (in the USA) by the James Beard Foundation in 2016. That was just months after the salted caramel chocolate brownie made by the wholesale Larder Baking Company, which Suzanne runs with her business partner, Caroline Styne (left), debuted at the West Hollywood Shack in two special Concretes. Coincidence? Perhaps!

Or maybe the team's three award-winning LA restaurants—Lucques, A.O.C., and Tavern had something to do with it. Or did her cookbooks, the now-classic *Sunday Suppers at Lucques* and *The A.O.C Cookbook,* influence the judges? No matter. Mark reached out to Suzanne and Caroline for that stellar brownie and never looked back.

Cofax

LOS ANGELES, CA

Yes, that was star baker Nicole Rucker (above, right), dropping off two glorious pies as big as your head to the kitchen of the West Hollywood Shake Shack just before the opening party; such is the community feeling here. After a storied rise as one of Los Angeles' best pastry chefs, with a notably long run at Gjusta, the Venice bakery connected with the restaurant, Gjelina, Nicole moved to Cofax as a partner. One goal: reinvent the donut. Cofax (the name is a mash-up of the Brooklyn/LA Dodgers' legendary pitcher, Sandy Koufax, and the notion of coffee on Fairfax, the central LA street where the shop is located) now features donuts such as honey sea salt and maple bacon.

Rucker says she savors the freedom to grow a culture where "I work harder but smile more!" With her right hand, Krystle Shelton (above, left), Rucker endlessly tastes and tests. "We're keeping a very open mind and with all that freedom to create, who knows where this will lead to?" Mark loves her spiced crumb cake donut, with amped up nutmeg and mace, and mixed it into the Rainbow Connection Concrete at WeHo.

Compartés

LOS ANGELES, CA

When Jonathan Grahm was 23, and without a whit of experience (at running a business or making chocolate, for example) he bought Compartés, his family's neighborhood candy store in Brentwood, California. "It was the biggest, best mistake I ever made," he recalls. "But I got into it." In a big way. Chocolate is Art! reads the neon sign in his two LA shops. "It was everything I love: Style! Design! Chocolate! I learned everything I needed from Google," he confesses. Grahm's idea was to create artisanal chocolates in astounding flavors and textures with a kind of elevated nostalgia, making childhood memories like S'mores and Donuts & Coffee newly hip. Grahm designs the imaginative packages and writes the stories that wrap the chocolates, too. He does his own marketing and PR, figuring out distribution for some 300 outlets across the country, and in Japan as well. No wonder Mark chose Compartés Liquid Gold dark chocolate chunks for the LA Edition of the classic Shack Attack Concrete.

Westbury, NY Freestanding in the heart of a Long Island shopping center, this Shack features recycled and sustainable materials, plus solar panels on the roof.

"We want our Shacks to seem like they've been part of their community forever. We constantly challenge ourselves. We can flex up or down: in a train station, in a park, in a stadium. Our sweet spot is balancing innovative design—architecture, seating, lighting—with lots of warmth that makes people feel really great."

—ANDREW McCAUGHAN, VP, DEVELOPMENT

Counter Evolution

NEW YORK, NY

"So here's a leap," says Jim Malone, a former cartoon producer and the original voice director for Pokémon. "I was obsessed with making a kitchen counter from a single wooden slab. Research led me to old bowling lane wood made from sturdy heart pine, the steel of the 19th century. I designed a few pieces for the Brooklyn Flea from that wood. My first sale was a big table for Starbuck's. When I met Randy in about 2010, he ordered tables for three Shacks at once." Counter Evolution's tables now appear in most Shacks, finished with a natural oil Jim developed instead of polyurethane.

Uhuru

BROOKLYN, NY

Bill Hilgendorf, left, and Jason Horvath, in their workroom, below, met in ceramics class at RISD, then founded Uhuru, their furniture design and fabrication company named for the Swahili word for "creativity."

From sprawling factory space in Red Hook, Brooklyn, that overlooks New York Harbor, the partners turn out metal-framed solid wood stools, chairs, tables, and more for Shake Shack as they have for years. "We are makers," Bill explains. "We have our hands on every part of the project." "Talk about sustainability," Jason adds. "One of the best ways to conserve resources is to make durable things that will last."

"Who ever wrote the rule that all Shacks must look alike?"

—DANNY MEYER

Battery Park City, NY A little secret about the glittery Shack tucked into the heart of New York's downtown financial district is that its details are all in "money green."

Dumbo, Brooklyn Reanimating existing space, as exemplified by the Shack retrofitted into the old brick buildings under the Brooklyn Bridge, is part of the Shack's mission.

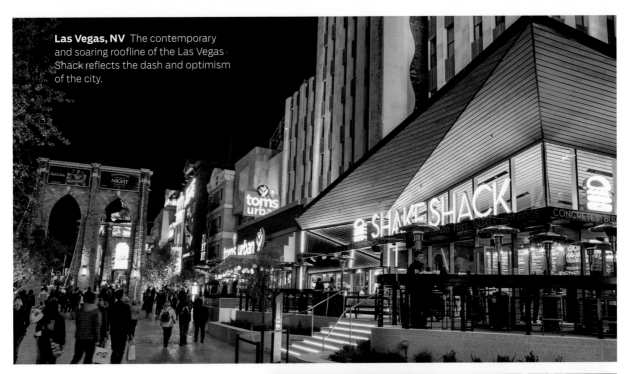

Las Vegas, NV The contemporary and soaring roofline of the Las Vegas Shack reflects the dash and optimism of the city.

Philadelphia, PA Center City Philly's Sansom Shack proudly participated in the city's robust Mural Arts program that has transformed the city.

Citi Field, NY Opening a Shack at Citi Field in Queens, home of the NY Mets, in 2009, was a test of the brand's flexibility.

Meiji-Jingu Gaien Park, Tokyo
Michael, Randy, Mark, and Megan
join our Japanese partner Anthony
Tsunoda, at the blessing before
opening the first Japanese Shack.

At Home Abroad

"We're not always looking for the busiest
street corner," says Michael Kark. "We're
looking for the best place for our brand to
have a soul." Expanding internationally
through partnerships in Europe, the Middle
East, and now Asia, Kark tries to understand
"what will be the best cultural fit for us.
Because we're a really big brand but we're
actually a very small team."

Opening in Tokyo in 2015, with priests
leading a traditional Shinto ceremony to
bless the health and growth of the business,

was a moving event for the home team.

"I always wake up on the morning of an
opening and worry 'What if nobody comes?'"
Randy admits. As it turned out, people had
slept out the night before in the park, where
the Shack was built among the gingko trees.

"The opportunity to have our people travel
abroad, to train our local teams in the values
of hospitality, and then," as Kark explains,
"cycle them back into the pool and then have
them spread the word—it's an incredible
employment incentive."

Covent Garden, London (above) is an excellent example of retrofitting a 21st-century Shack into 19th-century space.

Qatar It's a lively scene at the Shack in the Villaggio Mall in Doha.

"Our brand is universal. It crosses borders and political tensions. Locals are thrilled that we take the time to learn their culture, understand their food, and present local flavors."

—MICHAEL KARK, VP, LICENSED BUSINESS

Chapter

8

Chills & Thrills

Cumberland Dairy

NEW YORK, NY

Our frozen custard adventure began with the dairy food scientist Barry Jones and his son, Andrew, who helped us develop our original custard base. Today, it's made by Cumberland, a company with an American story similar to that of so many of our suppliers. In the 1930s, Charles Catalana turned a part-time job delivering milk in rural New Jersey into a regional dairy-processing powerhouse that is one of three producers across the country who process our custard base that's shipped to Shacks nationwide. Cumberland Dairy's milk comes from family-farming co-ops within a 90-mile radius of Bridgeton, New Jersey. And like these happy grazers, right, most dairy cows are Holsteins.

Dairy farmers working with the still family-owned company's pledge not to use the growth hormone rBST on their cows, and as each milk shipment arrives at the processing facility, it's tested for antibiotics. Cumberland then assembles Shack's custard base with milk, cream, sugar, and cage-free eggs.

Coffee Fair Shake
MAKES 1

Put 1½ cups Frozen Vanilla Custard
(*page 214*), 2 tablespoons
strong cold espresso (something
great like Stumptown), and
⅓ cup milk in a blender.
Blend on high until smooth.

Vanilla Shake
MAKES 1

Put 1½ cups Frozen Vanilla
Custard (*page 214*) and ½ cup
milk in a blender. Blend on
high until smooth.

Here Come the Shack Shakes...

It couldn't be easier to whip frozen custard into a tall cold drink.

Black & White Shake

MAKES 1

Put 1½ cups Frozen Vanilla Custard
(page 214), 2 tablespoons
Fudge Sauce *(page 221)*, and
⅓ cup milk in a blender. Blend
on high until smooth.

Salted Caramel Shake

MAKES 1

Put 1½ cups Frozen Vanilla Custard
(page 214), 2 tablespoons
Salted Caramel Sauce *(page 205)*,
and ⅓ cup milk in a blender.
Blend on high until smooth.

All our shakes have the same ratio of ingredients, so it's easy to customize your flavors. And each recipe makes one 16-ounce shake. We always begin with the same amount of custard: 1½ cups. Then, we add ½ cup milk. And blend. That's it!

For other flavored shakes, add 2 tablespoons of your favorite sauce or puree, and use ⅓ cup milk. So now you know our secrets.

Making a Shack Shake (at home!)

Here's the master plan; substitute your favorite premium ice cream, we won't tell!

1. Assemble the ingredients, Vanilla Frozen Custard, Salted Caramel Sauce, apple puree, salt, and milk.

2. Transfer all ingredients to a blender and blend well.

3. Pour the blended shake into a glass and repeat for as many shakes as you want!

4. Sip your creation, like this Salted Caramel Apple Shake, slowly to make it last.

Salted Caramel Apple Shake

MAKES 1

Our step-by-step method for making this luscious shake is detailed on the opposite page.

To 1½ cups custard in a blender, add 3 tablespoons apple puree (we order our fruit purees from perfectpuree.com), 2 tablespoons Salted Caramel Sauce, a pinch of salt, and ⅓ cup milk and blend.

Salted Caramel Sauce

MAKES 1½ CUPS

Salted caramel is like a Bugs Bunny cartoon; it appeals to everyone, kids and adults alike, but for different reasons: kids like its sweetness, we love its salty edge. The sauce is so good as a topping for a scoop of ice cream, great in a shake, left, or how about in a Concrete with vanilla custard, some chopped banana, and bits of shortbread cookies for crunch? Just saying . . .

1 cup sugar	2 teaspoons sea salt
1 cup heavy cream	

1. Put sugar and ⅓ cup water into a deep medium pot. Swirl the pot to moisten the sugar. Bring to a boil over medium-high heat, gently swirling the pot often to help dissolve the sugar into a clear syrup.

2. Boil the syrup until it smokes and just begins to turn a deep caramel brown, 5 to 8 minutes. The syrup will continue to brown very quickly. Be careful it doesn't burn. When the syrup is uniformly brown, quickly and carefully add the cream, stirring until the sauce is smooth and returns to a boil, about 1 minute. Remove the pot from the heat. Stir in the salt. Caramel Sauce will keep, covered and refrigerated, for up to 1 week.

@tiarasamosir

"Our goal is very specific: end childhood hunger in the United States. The funds Shake Shack raises every year in its Great American Shake Sale have turbocharged our efforts. For each dollar we spend, we get 10 meals for hungry kids."

**—BILLY SHORE,
NO KID HUNGRY,
SHARE OUR STRENGTH**

Raspberry Fromage Blanc Shake

MAKES 1

Put 1½ cups Frozen Vanilla Custard *(page 214)* in a blender, add 2 tablespoons fromage blanc (or Greek yogurt), ¼ cup fresh raspberries, and ½ cup milk and blend.

Blueberry Lemon Curd Shake

MAKES 1

Put 1½ cups Frozen Vanilla Custard *(page 214)* in a blender, add 2 tablespoons lemon curd, ½ cup fresh blueberries, and ¼ cup milk and blend.

Chocolate Peppermint Shake

MAKES 1

1. Put 1½ cups Frozen Chocolate Custard *(page 215)* in a blender, add ½ cup milk, and ⅛ teaspoon peppermint extract.

2. For garnish you'll need lots of whipped cream and 1 teaspoon finely chopped chocolate peppermint candies (we like Williams-Sonoma's Chocolate Peppermint Sticks).

Pumpkin Spice Shake

MAKES 1

This shake was made for autumn days. Add all the ingredients to a blender and mix it up. Or, use a large scoop of filling from your favorite pumpkin pie.

1½ **cups Frozen Vanilla Custard** *(page 214)*	⅛ **teaspoon ground clove**
⅓ **cup milk**	⅛ **teaspoon ground nutmeg**
2 **tablespoons pumpkin puree**	⅛ **teaspoon ground allspice**
1 **teaspoon ground cinnamon**	
½ **teaspoon ground ginger**	

Chocolate Shake

MAKES 1

Put 1½ cups Frozen Chocolate Custard *(page 215)* and ½ cup milk in a blender. Blend on high until smooth. Serve in a tall cold glass.

One Stop Choc

BALTHAZAR COOKIE

The New York bakery (next to the famous restaurant) that produces this chocolate shortbread cookie has production in New Jersey, perfect for our NJ Shacks. Marshmallow sauce says S'mores; hazelnuts add crunch.

CHOCOLATE SPRINKLES

Beware! Most sprinkles are waxy concoctions. We found the purest, most chocolately sprinkles at Guittard, in San Francisco.

MARSHMALLOW SAUCE

Mark grew up on sundaes at his local Friendly's, where his fave was Reese's Pieces peanut butter with marshmallow topping. Hence this marshmallow sauce that adds a flavorful vanilla note, plus its flat white color enhances the chocolate.

CHOCOLATE CUSTARD

Two flavors of chocolate make far more luscious custard than one. Our custard recipe (page 215), combines 70% bittersweet plus unsweetened cocoa.

SHAKE SHACK®

Berry Patch

SHORTBREAD

This Concrete has the vibe of a berry pie, and shortbread, with its wonderful texture and mild buttery flavor note, acts as the crust. It's one of our favorite mix-ins as a blank canvas that holds together all the other ingredients.

a Concrete

Township Toffee

VANILLA CUSTARD

Vanilla adds intense flavor to any ingredient it touches; use the best quality you can find (*recipe page 214*).

CHOCOLATE TOFFEE

Our toffee is a magical combination of pure butter, sugar, fine French chocolate, and sea salt. Use the best you can find.

MALT POWDER

Malt is a classic soda shop staple that adds a touch of bitterness and a crispy texture. In Kuwait we use malt for a Sandstorm Concrete that looks like sand dunes.

BLUEBERRY LIME JAM

New Jersey is berry country, and we always look for people making the best local jams to pair with the vanilla custard for our local deconstructed pie à la mode Concretes.

SALTED CARAMEL SAUCE

This is our generation's go-to topping, and kids love it, too. With its bittersweet, smoky, salty flavor, it's perfect drizzled over both chocolate and vanilla custard, or fruit, or in a shake (*recipe page 205*).

Making Frozen Custard *(at home!)*

It may seem tricky, but you can really do this!

1. Whisk milk and cream into egg yolk and sugar mixture.

2. When the mixture's thick enough to coat the back of a spoon . . .

3. Strain into a bowl and add the salt and vanilla.

4. Cool the custard base in a bowl of ice cubes and chill for 4 hours.

5. Churn the custard in an ice cream maker following manufacturer's directions.

Frozen Vanilla Custard

MAKES ABOUT 1 QUART

This is it! The master recipe for most of our Concretes and milkshakes, tweaked so you can make it at home. Frozen custard is simply freshly made ice cream with a higher butterfat and egg yolk content. Because we make ours fresh all day in small batches, our custard stays creamy and dense, its flavor heightened by the best vanilla we can find. A favorite is Nielsen-Massey pure vanilla extract from Waukegan, Illinois.

5 egg yolks	Pinch of salt
½ cup sugar	1 teaspoon good quality pure vanilla extract
1½ cups heavy cream	
1½ cups milk	

1. Put the egg yolks and sugar into a heavy medium saucepan and whisk until smooth. Whisk in the cream and milk. Cook over medium heat, stirring frequently with a wooden spoon, until the custard reaches a temperature of 170°F on an instant-read thermometer or is thick enough to coat the back of the spoon.

2. Strain the custard into a medium bowl. Stir in the salt and vanilla. Set that bowl into a larger bowl filled with ice, then stir the custard frequently until it has cooled. Cover the custard and refrigerate it until completely chilled, about 4 hours.

3. Churn the custard in an ice cream maker following the manufacturer's instructions. Scoop the custard into a quart container with a lid, cover, and store in the freezer for at least 2 hours, until firm. Custard can be kept up to a month in the freezer, but we prefer to eat it within 24 hours!

Frozen Chocolate Custard

MAKES ABOUT 1 QUART

The obvious determining factor in this recipe is the quality of the chocolate. We seek out and use craft chocolate like Mast Brothers *(page 223)* and Compartés *(page 191)* wherever possible. It does make a difference. We also love the chocolate from Guittard and TCHO, both from San Francisco.

¼ cup unsweetened cocoa

2 ounces 70% bittersweet chocolate, cut into small pieces

5 egg yolks

½ cup sugar

1½ cups heavy cream

1½ cups milk

Pinch of salt

1. Set the cocoa and chopped bittersweet chocolate aside in a large heatproof bowl.

2. Put the egg yolks and sugar into a heavy medium saucepan and whisk until smooth. Gradually whisk in the cream and milk. Cook over medium heat, stirring frequently with a wooden spoon, until the custard reaches a temperature of 170ºF on an instant-read thermometer or is thick enough to coat the back of the spoon.

3. Pour the warm custard into the large bowl with the 2 chocolates and let it sit for a minute to melt the chocolate. Add salt and stir well, smoothly incorporating all the chocolate.

4. Strain the custard into a medium bowl. Set that bowl into a larger bowl filled with ice, then stir the custard frequently until it has cooled. Cover the custard and refrigerate it until completely chilled, about 4 hours.

5. Churn the custard in an ice cream maker following the manufacturer's instructions. Scoop the ice cream into a quart container with a lid, cover, and store in the freezer. Custard can be kept up to a month in the freezer, but we prefer to eat it within 24 hours!

Pie Oh My Concrete
SERVES 2

Make this Concrete with whatever pie's the apple of your eye. It's one of our favorites, maybe because it hearkens back to the classic American pie and burger combo. A well-constructed pie adds yummy texture and jammy consistency to the frozen custard.

3-4 scoops Frozen Vanilla Custard *(page 214)*

1 slice blueberry or mixed berry pie, cut into ½-inch pieces

1 cup whipped cream, optional

1. Spoon the frozen vanilla custard into a medium bowl. Add the pie. Cover with wrap and transfer the bowl to the freezer for at least 15 minutes and as long as 2 hours.

2. When ready to serve, gently mash ingredients together with a wooden spoon until just combined. Spoon the Concretes into 2 dessert dishes, top with whipped cream, if using, and serve.

To make a Pecan Pie Oh My, just substitute a nice slice of good pecan pie for the berry pie and enjoy!

LOCAL HERO

Four & Twenty Blackbirds
BROOKLYN, NY

Emily Elsen (left) and her sister, Melissa, have a storybook American tale. The girls grew up in the South Dakota town of Hecla (population 230), where their family owned a homestyle restaurant and their grandmother, Liz, just happened to be a famous pie baker. After art school in New York and London (Emily), and a degree in finance (Melissa), the girls moved into an old house in Brooklyn. "Whenever we thought about a business to start, it always came back to pies," Emily remembers. "Every time I made a pie, people would flip out. They said I had a gift!"

The sisters had a simple goal: Make the best pies. In 2009, they found a funky shop space in Gowanus, Brooklyn, renovated it with friends, and sold out as soon as they opened. "We were in over our heads right away." Soon afterward, they met the folks from Shake Shack, and began supplying pies for Pie Oh My Concretes.

Ron Palmese, Vicki Shih, Phil Crawford, and Josh Omin lead so many of the team members and processes that make the Shack hum behind the scenes.

H&F Bread Co.

ATLANTA, GA

Award-winning chef Linton Hopkins and his wife, Gina, a sommelier, are household names on the Atlanta fine dining restaurant scene, where they run among others, the renowned Restaurant Eugene and Holman & Finch Public House, for which their H & F Bread Co. is named. Started to feed their restaurant company, H & F has gained renown in its own right, turning out artisanal breads and pastries such as these pecan pies that Shake Shack mixes into Pecan Pie Oh My Concretes in Atlanta, here proudly shown by Fallon Parks (left) in the cozy, sweet-smelling shop tucked into the front of the bakery.

Shack Attack

SERVES 2

This Concrete has been our #1 seller since it was first served at Madison Square Park in 2004. Only the mix-ins have evolved. As we enter new communities, we reach out to the best local purveyors. In London, it's chocolate hazelnut brownies from Fergus Henderson's St. JOHN Bakery and paul.a.young's craft chocolate chunks. In Tokyo, the brownies are from Dominique Ansel's bakery. In LA, we mix Suzanne Goin's salted caramel chocolate brownie from her Larder Baking Co. with Compartés dark chocolate chunks. Make your own with your favorite small batch brownies and chocolate.

3 to 4 scoops Frozen Chocolate Custard *(page 215)*

2 tablespoons Fudge Sauce

½ cup brownie cut into small pieces

3 tablespoons Mast Brothers or other craft chocolate, broken into chunks

2 tablespoons chocolate sprinkles

1. Spoon the frozen chocolate custard into a medium bowl. Add the fudge sauce, brownies, and chocolate. Cover with wrap and transfer the bowl to the freezer for at least 15 minutes and as long as 2 hours.

2. When ready to serve, gently mash ingredients together with a wooden spoon until just combined. Spoon the Concretes into 2 dessert dishes, top with the sprinkles, and serve.

Put cream, milk, sugar, and butter into a large saucepan and bring just to a boil over medium heat. Add the chocolate and cook, stirring often, until chocolate melts. Remove pan from heat. Let fudge sauce cool, stirring occasionally. Fudge sauce will keep, covered and refrigerated, for up to 1 week.

Fudge Sauce

MAKES 2 CUPS

⅓ cup heavy cream

⅔ cup milk

¼ cup sugar

2 tablespoons unsalted butter

1 cup bittersweet chocolate, finely chopped

Dominique Ansel

NEW YORK AND TOKYO

As Dominique tells it, he arrived in New York from Paris in 2006 with two suitcases to be executive pastry chef for Daniel Boulud at Daniel. By 2011, he'd opened his own shop in SoHo, where, in 2013, he launched the Cronut, that marriage of croissant and donut that rocketed to worldwide fame.

Mark, who admires Dominique's "creativity, warmth, and uncanny ability to push culinary boundaries," asked him to make a Cronut Concrete for charity. Dominique's Concrete had a base of the Shack's butter caramel frozen custard with cinnamon sugar Cronut holes. When Tokyo Shacks opened, Dominique had a bakery there, too: Tokyo Shack Attack Concretes feature his milk chocolate popcorn brownie.

LOCAL HERO

Fergus Henderson

LONDON, UK

How the chef made famous by his book *The Whole Beast, Nose to Tail Eating,* can make what Mark calls the "Best. Brownie. Ever." is one of life's sweet mysteries. But Fergus, whose London restaurant, St. JOHN, is a tribute to elemental yet elegant food, just knows what good is. St. JOHN Bakery makes intensely flavorful goodies. That chocolate hazelnut brownie and their brown sugar biscuit star in Concretes at the London Shacks, and at Cardiff, Wales, too. That's Henderson, below front, hard at work at their French vineyard, backed by his St. JOHN partner, Trevor Gulliver, left, and winemaker/partner, Benjamin Darnault.

Mast Brothers

BROOKLYN, NY

"We're a chocolate company," says Rick Mast, above left, with his brother, Michael, in their Brooklyn shop/factory. "With so much hate and divisiveness in the world, you can't go wrong coming down on the side of love." Since 2007, the brothers' dream was to "start a family food business with chocolate as the focus that blends into architecture, design, art, and music." They obsess over the proper blending of cacao beans from small farm cooperatives while at the same time focusing on such expansion as moving into a vast space in the newly reimagined neighborhood of Downtown Los Angeles.

"We had a lot of respect for Danny and Mark and bonded over our love of good food," says Michael. "Our relationship is super-collaborative. The Mast Brothers Shake Shack Buttermilk Chocolate bar in its signature wrapper is sold at Shacks and used as an ingredient in Concretes.

Staple Concrete

SERVES 2

Staple Pigeon is a hotter than hot menswear company that elevates streetwear to cult status. Working with Jeff Staple, Mark's challenge was to create a Concrete that looked like a pigeon (Staple's mascot) and tasted like a dream. To Mark, pigeon gray equaled black sesame donuts from Doughnut Plant; to mirror a pigeons' pink feet, Mark conjured up raspberry preserves.

3 to 4 scoops Frozen Vanilla Custard *(page 214)*

1 **black sesame donut or other cake donut, broken into ½-inch pieces**

¼ **cup red raspberry preserves**

1. Spoon the frozen custard into a medium bowl. Add the donuts and raspberry preserves. Cover with wrap and transfer the bowl to the freezer for at least 15 minutes and as long as 2 hours.

2. When ready to serve, gently mash ingredients together with a wooden spoon until just combined. Spoon the Concretes into 2 dessert dishes and serve immediately.

LOCAL HERO

Jeff Staple

NEW YORK, NY

The tiny pink rivet on the pocket of his black Staple Pigeon shorts is the clue to fashion designer/manufacturer Jeff Staple's aesthetic. It's what put raspberry preserves in the Staple Concrete launched at Madison Square Park that, along with a Staple-designed T-shirt and glasses, sold out in about 30 seconds. Google staplepigeon.com for an idea of how pigeons—and contemporary culture—work their magic. Staple says of his relationship with Shake Shack: "We bonded over our mutual respect and our links to New York City culture."

Rainbow Concrete

SERVES 2

Donuts and Concretes are perfect mates and the Rainbow's a big favorite for kids' birthday parties. We created a special version, the Rainbow Connection, for the opening of our West Hollywood Shack, combining Nicole Rucker's spice crumb donut from Cofax with Jessica Koslow's Seascape Strawberry & Rose Geranium jam from Sqirl. In Philadelphia, we use Federal Donuts' French toast donut, and in Chicago, it's a salted caramel old-fashioned donut from Glazed and Infused.

3 to 4 scoops Frozen Vanilla Custard *(page 214)*

1 spiced crumb donut or other cake donut, broken into ½-inch pieces

¼ cup strawberry preserves

2 tablespoons rainbow sprinkles

1. Spoon the frozen vanilla custard into a medium bowl. Add the donuts and strawberry preserves. Cover with wrap and transfer the bowl to the freezer for at least 15 minutes and as long as 2 hours.

2. When ready to serve, gently mash ingredients together with a wooden spoon until just combined. Spoon the Concretes into 2 dessert dishes, top with rainbow sprinkles, and serve immediately.

Federal Donuts

PHILADELPHIA, PA

They admit to knowing nothing about making donuts when the five friends gathered in Philadelphia in 2011. But they did know about cooking and serving food. Michael Solomonov, far left, and his business partner, Steven Cook, far right, had opened the already-famous modern Israeli restaurant, Zahav, in 2008. Bobby Logue, next to Steve, ran a hip coffee shop, Bodhi Coffee, in South Philly, often with Tom Henneman, next to Mike, now Fed Nuts' general manager. Felicia D'Ambrosio is a social media maven.

Bobby found "a greasy, pizza parlor down on Second Street." The five became partners, expanding their Federal Donuts shops that serve both hot fresh and fancy glazed donuts, in flavors like grapefruit and pomegranate-Nutella. And since there is all that hot oil, they make fried chicken too, dusted with exotic spices.

Philly Shacks serve Fed Nuts mix-ins such as the French toast fancy donut in our Declaration of Donuts Concrete.

Shack Floats

A float is the simplest thing, but it's exciting because the flavors keep changing. First there's the impact of the bubbly soda, then, as the custard melts into the drink, every sip and every bite is different and fun. Here are just two examples. But how about swapping out the soda for Brooklyn Brewery's Chocolate Stout? Add grape soda and it's a Purple Cow. The combinations are endless.

Orange Cream Float

MAKES 1

Pour 12 ounces cold Fanta orange soda into a tall wide chilled 24-ounce glass. Gently add 2 scoops Frozen Vanilla Custard *(page 214)*.

Root Beer Float

MAKES 1

Pour 12 ounces cold Abita or other fine root beer into a tall wide chilled 24-ounce glass. Gently add 2 scoops Frozen Vanilla Custard *(page 214)*.

LOCAL HERO

Abita Root Beer

COVINGTON, LA

Clearly, Danny's memory of the old-fashioned draft root beer (with its secret recipe!) served at his teen hangout, Fitz's in St. Louis, led the search for it to this craft brewery on the North Shore of Lake Pontchartrain, across from New Orleans.

Abita makes bright root beer that's served on tap at most Shacks. It has that authentic draft root beer smell and flavor of fresh herbs, vanilla, yucca, and Louisiana cane sugar, involving no corn syrup or other artificial ingredients. The magic, it's said, comes from the healing powers of the spring water they use from an artisanal well in Abita Springs.

@puppynamedcharlie

"Sometimes the dog makes the family dining decisions."

—RANDY GARUTTI

Pooch-ini

MAKES 1

When we opened in Madison Square Park, so many of our customers showed up after taking their pets to the Park's dog run that we thought it would only be good hospitality to offer something to those hungry, thirsty dogs, too. Hence the Pooch-ini. We make ours with Bocce's all-natural ShackBurger Dog Biscuits.

Put 2 tablespoons smooth peanut butter in a dog dish. Add 1 or 2 scoops Frozen Vanilla Custard (page 214). Break some dog biscuits *(page 232)* in pieces and scatter over the custard.

"We love dogs! This goes back to being born in a park where you could come have a burger and let your pet loose at the dog run. Our Shacks love to host pet adoption organizations like Badass Brooklyn Animal Rescue, Bobbi and the Strays, and PAWS. No sensible dog would sniff at our dog biscuits and dog-friendly dessert, the Pooch-ini."

—EDWIN BRAGG, VP, MARKETING & COMMUNICATIONS

@bingodalgal

Bocce's PB & Banana Dog Biscuits

MAKES ABOUT 3 DOZEN SMALL BISCUITS

This is one version of the healthy dog biscuits made by Andrea Tovar at Bocce's Bakery. For more treats, check out boccesbakery.com.

2 bananas (about 12 ounces), peeled and cut into large pieces

⅓ cup peanut butter

3 cups oat flour

1. Preheat the oven to 350ºF. Put the bananas and peanut butter in a food processor and purée until creamy, about 1 minute. Add the oat flour and process until the dough comes together in a ball, about 1 minute.

2. On a lightly oat-floured surface, roll out the dough to about ¼ inch thick. Cut into shapes using any cookie cutter. Dip the cookie cutter in the oat flour with each cut. Work from the center of the rolled-out dough out to the edges, cutting shapes close to prevent extra rerolling. Place cookies 1 inch apart on ungreased cookie sheets. Bake until golden, about 25 minutes.

LOCAL HERO

Bocce's Bakery

NEW YORK, NY

Named appropriately for baker/owner Andrea Tovar's dog, Bocce's began when Andrea discovered that most dog treats were filled with chemicals. An organic baker, Andrea, below left, with her sister,

Natalia, began baking healthy biscuits out of a tiny New York apartment.

Andrea says she'd always loved Shake Shack and was surprised when she took Bocce to Madison Square Park for his Pooch-ini that its dog treats were pretty ordinary. A random email resulted in a meeting with Mark Rosati, where "he eagerly tasted every dog biscuit I made." Together they developed biscuits with "human-grade" ingredients, wheat-free, packed with fruits and vegetables. (ShackBurger Biscuits use Pat LaFrieda's beef!) Shacks began selling Andrea's Bag O' Bones. When the first London Shack opened in 2013, Andrea found a London baker to partner with, to source and bake locally.

Acknowledgments

First thanks go to our Culinary Director, Mark Rosati, whose talented hands touched every recipe in this book and whose food sensibility informs everything we serve. And to our Culinary and Supply Chain team who endlessly dream up better ways to make Shake Shack taste great: especially Jeff Amoscato, Lisa Kartzman, Alison Oesterle, Gillian Ortiz, Vafa Mansouri, Gary Schwartz, and John Berberich.

To the incredible team who made this book: the talented Dorothy Kalins, whose passion for translating the Shack story to the page is unmatched, the brilliant designer Don Morris, with us every step of the way, indefatigable photo editor, Amy Lundeen, to the gifted photographers, Christopher Hirsheimer and Melissa Hamilton. To Roger Sherman, Ashley Giddens, and Adam Segaller.

At Potter, we thank our champions Rica Allannic and Marysarah Quinn. Plus, Aaron Wehner, Doris Cooper, Derek Gullino, Christine Tanigawa, Mark McCauslin, Andrea Portanova, Neil Spitkovsky, Kelli Tokos, Kevin Sweeting, Jana Branson, and Kate Tyler.

To David Black for believing in this book even when there was only one Shack.

To our Marketing team who enhances the story of the Shack brand every day: especially Edwin Bragg, Cathie Urushibata, Laura Enoch, Jacqueline Gonzales.

Roxanne Dalere and Hailey Klingel for their diligent work behind the scenes for this book.

To our Operations and People teams who develop the culture that makes us extraordinary worldwide: especially Zach Koff, Peggy Rubenzer, Michael Kark, Mike Iaia, Jon Vandegrift, Elizabeth Watkins, Kevin Garry, Erik Hugley, Tom Hunton, Matt Meyer, Bryan Murphy, Alln Ng, Amanda Quintal, Mike Tuiach, Alexandra Valdes-Fauli, Michael Wang, Dave Yearwood, Sean Wagner, and Cathy Fendelman.

To our Development team who designs and builds our Shacks: especially Andrew McCaughan, Lou DeAngelis, Carren Ballenger, and Lily Jordan.

To our Finance, IT, and Legal teams, especially Josh Omin, Vicki Shih, Amy Mock, Jeannette Hill, Dana Chipouras, Phil Crawford, Giancarlo Fiorarancio, Cindy Ronson, and of course, Ron Palmese.

To Taylor DeLorenzo, who helped make the pages of this book better with every turn.

To our fans and their communities: Thanks for creating the gathering place that is Shake Shack.

To all of the artisans, farmers, designers, construction crews, partners, and suppliers who appear in this book and to those who don't: You inspire us.

To our Board of Directors: Bert Vivian, Jeff Flug, Jenna Lyons, Jon Sokoloff, Evan Guillemin, and Josh Silverman.

To our investors and shareholders, who believe in what we do, why we exist, and where we're going.

To Mohammed Alshaya, who believed in us long before everyone else.

To our global partners, who magically translate Shacks to their communities around the world.

To David Swinghamer: your wisdom, vision, and leadership through the key early years of Shake Shack built something truly special.

To Richard Coraine: RC, we all stand on your shoulders.

To Jeff Flug for believing in me and the possibilities of the Shack.

To PBB and MPR: for 20 years of love at USC that gave a little burger-joint the head start we didn't deserve.

To Danny Meyer: our founder, our inspiration. Because of you, there is a thing called Shake Shack, and the world is a way more interesting place.

To Maria: You are everything. Natural progression forever. And to our children, Caleb, Connor, and Keira, who light our life.

RANDY GARUTTI

To my family, especially my parents, Marie and Robert, for all your love, faith, and inspiration.

To Laura, for all your wonderful suport, inspiration, and understanding.

To Randy, Jon, Eliz, Alex, Jenny, Mike, Amanda, Zach, Jeff, Gillian, and Allison, for always inspiring, teaching, and driving me to achieve my best every day since I joined Shake Shack.

To Tom Colicchio and John Schaefer, for taking a chance and inviting me into your kitchen back in 2004.

MARK ROSATI

Credits

ROGER SHERMAN: 16 (bottom left); 30 (top and right), 31 (top right); 52, 58, 59, 95, 98, 122 (left), 158, 160 (4); 161 (3); 187 (inset), 193 (3), 218 (top), 219 (2), 223 (2), 227 (2). **MARY COSTA:** 2, 3, 28, 110, 157, 182 (top), 183 (left 3), 185 (top and bottom left), 198. **EVAN SUNG:** 80 (bottom), 81 (bottom), 82 (bottom), 83 (bottom), 84 (bottom), 85, 104, 134 (bottom), 135, 205. **WONHO FRANK LEE:** 7, 169, 178, 184 (bottom). **THOMAS DALLAL:** 8, 14 (right). **COURTESY STEAK 'N SHAKE®:** 16. **RANDALL HYMAN:** 16 (bottom right). **NOTLEY HAWKINS:** 17 (top left). **COURTESY MISSOURI DIVISION OF TOURISM:** 17 (bottom left). **KAHLIL NELSON:** 17 (bottom center). **CITIZEN OF THE PLANET/ALAMY STOCK PHOTO:** 17 (bottom right). **SHAKE SHACK:** 18, 21 (2), 72, 99, 101, 118, 124 (left), 125 (left); 154; 174 (bottom); 176, 181 (left), 195 (bottom left), 196, 197 (3), 231 (top). **ROBERT JACOB LERMA:** 19. **COURTESY RICHARD CORAINE:** 20. **PAULA SCHER/ PENTAGRAM:** 24. **INTERFOTO/ALAMY STOCK PHOTO:** 30 (left). **GARY WARNIMONT/ALAMY STOCK PHOTO:** 31 (top left). **EVERETT COLLECTION INC./ALAMY STOCK PHOTO:** 31 (bottom left). **STARS AND STRIPES/ALAMY STOCK PHOTO:** 31 (center). **EVAAN KHERAJ:** 31 (right). **JON MULLEN/ISTOCK:** 32 (top). **COURTESY JEFFREY AMOSCATO:** 32 (bottom). **CHRISTOPHER ELWELL/SHUTTERSTOCK:** 33. **COURTESY MARK ROSATI:** 36, 108 (bottom), 222 (bottom). **COURTESY MARTIN'S POTATO ROLLS:** 42. **COURTESY LUCKY LEE:** 49 (top and center). **COURTESY NIMAN RANCH:** 55 (3). **DANIEL KRIEGER:** 63 (right), 64. **COURTESY JOHN FOLSE:** 71 (right). **YUXI LIU:** 73. **ESTO/PETER MAUSS:** 74 (left), 194 (top). **CHRISTIAN HANSEN/NEW YORK TIMES/REDUX:** 74 (right). **RAFE ABROOK PHOTOGRAPHY:** 75. **COURTESY FROG'S LEAP:** 76 (3). **COURTESY EDWIN BRAGG:** 79 (4), 81 (top); 134 (top). **GABRIELE STABILE:** 80 (top). **MARCO GROB:** 82 (top). **MADELEINE HILL:** 83 (top). **PAOLO TERZI:** 84 (top). **COURTESY VIENNA BEEF:** 88 (2). © **SEPS** licensed by Curtis Licensing Indianapolis, IN. All rights reserved: 107. **SEAN COOLEY:** 108 (top). **COURTESY PAUL KAHAN/DEREK RICHMOND:** 109. **TORU KOMETANI:** 113. **CHRIS ALFONSO:** 116, 120, 156. **GALDONES PHOTOGRAPHY:** 121. **AUDRA MELTON:** 122 (right 3), 123 (left and bottom 3). **KIMBERLY ABUAJAH:** 123 (top right). **COURTESY WATERKEEPER ALLIANCE:** 124 (right). **ALLAN NG:** 125 (right). © **2015 NYSE GROUP, INC.:** 126, 127; images of NYSE Group, Inc., some of which are a federally registered service mark, are used with permission of NYSE Group, Inc., and its affiliated companies. Neither NYSE Group, Inc., nor its affiliated companies recommend or make any representation as to possible benefits from any securities or investments. **COURTESY LAMB WESTON:** 136 (2), 137 (bottom). **RICHARD EBERT:** 137. **PAUL WINCH-FURNESS:** 148 (top). **BONDFIRE MEDIA RELATIONS & CONSULTING:** 159. **SEB OLIVER/GETTY IMAGES:** 162, 163. **HANNAH HUDSON PHOTOGRAPHY:** 174 (top). **JAMES JOHN JETEL:** 181 (right). **HOLLY LISS:** 182 (bottom). **RYAN TANAKA:** 183 (bottom right). **KAMRAN SHUAKAT:** 192. **STUDIO SSMC:** 194 (bottom). **EDISON GRAFF:** 195 (top). **NICOLE FRANZEN:** 195 (bottom right). **COURTESY CUMBERLAND DAIRY:** 200, 201. **LAM THUY VO:** 222 (top). **DOROTHY HONG:** 224 (right). **COURTESY ABITA BREWING COMPANY, LLC:** 228. **COURTESY BOCCE'S BAKERY:** 232.

INSTAGRAM:
@beeblegum, Bianca Davies: 12.
@whitneytravels, Whitney Tressel, 25.
@tishacherry, Tisha Saravitaya: 86.
@concoquere, Bernard Lin: 94.
@janelikesme, Jane Chung: 115.
@beingdave, Dave Dettloff: 128.
@the_m_o_m, Mickey Fuertes: 131.
@evan5ps for @epitomeatl. Creative Director @martinamcflyy: 142.
@benononsense, Gina DeNezzo Photogaphy. Roxanne White, Associate Creative Director, Kaplow Communications: 149.
@tiarasamosir, Aqil Raharjo: 206.
@puppynamedcharlie, Paige Chernick: 230.
@bingodalgal, Jessica Herrington: 231 (bottom).

Index

Note: Page references in *italics* indicate photographs.